GRACE RUNNER

BY
MARK MAYNARD

GRACE RUNNER

Copyright © 2014 by Mark Maynard

SOFTBACK EDITION

All rights reserved. No part of this book may be reproduced or transmitted in any form or by any means without written permission of the author.

ISNB: 978-0-9887319-6-7

Published by:

RIGHT EYE GRAPHICS
P.O. Box 5071
Ashland, Kentucky 41105-5071
606.393.4197
www.RightEyeGraphics.com

TABLE OF CONTENTS

1. Thrills and Chills... 11
2. Running in the wrong direction 27
3. 'You can't get high enough' 43
4. Connecting as disciples 55
5. Laying the groundwork 65
6. Turning it over to God 79
7. The mission 85
8. The unsung heroes 97
9. A moment to remember 103
10. Bringing a family together 113
11. Results of mission
    (how you can help) 117
12. A final word 123
13. Amy's diary 127

FOREWORD

When the first six months of this Amy For Africa mission came to an end with Amy Compston finishing second in the Nashville 50-mile Ultra Marathon on November 2, 2013, it became a time of looking back on what was truly a spiritual journey.

I have been a Christian for 45 years and have always tried to talk the talk and walk the walk. I have served in church leadership roles, taught Sunday School, been the Sunday School director, served as chairman of the deacons, volunteered whenever asked, led the music in services and tried to encourage a brother or sister whenever they needed it. But never in my life of trying to follow in the footsteps of Jesus Christ had He taken me to this spiritual place. In all honesty, this was a spiritual high for me in every way.

The six months leading up to the Ultra Marathon was full of miracles. We watched lives being changed and we saw God working without us even asking. We saw him open wallets and purses when we went to speak in churches without ever mentioning an offering. We were being used by Almighty God in a powerful way and it was amazing. It was so humbling to think He chose us to participate in this mission. Why? How did it happen? I had barely known Amy and her husband, Chris, for a year, but we developed a bond of Chris-

FOREWORD

tian friendship during these six months that can only be forged by God. I have been writing for most of my life but find it hard to put into words what has happened through this Amy For Africa mission journey. I am awestruck and amazed at what He has accomplished through us.

I started writing "Grace Runner" immediately after returning from Nashville, putting other projects aside, because of the importance it had taken in my life. The Amy For Africa mission had become a passion. My wife, Beth, saw a difference in me, too, as this was unfolding before our very eyes. She is the most dedicated Christian woman I have ever known and she jumped into the work because she wants to be where God is working. It is that simple. We remain best friends today with Chris and Amy Compston and watch as they keep growing into strong young adults who have put Christ at the head of the household. What a difference it has made in their lives. I hope they have learned from us even a little of what we learned from them.

Writing this book about Amy For Africa became increasingly more difficult because it was abundantly clear God was not finished with it. As this book is being completed, Chris and Amy are in the midst of running eight marathons in eight months and the Amy For Africa mission remains strong as ever. They impress with their athletic skills of running but are more impressive as young Christians who are on fire for God. It is a contagious kind of fire that has spread to others as well, both young and old. We have learned that our little world here in Ashland, Kentucky, is surrounded by many good Christian people who want to be part of something exciting. Amy For Africa provided that excitement and they wanted to be part of it. What a blessing to watch God work in churches throughout our area

FOREWORD

as we crossed denominational walls and did what He commands us all to do: Go Tell!

Here are two other lessons we learned: God does not make mistakes and there are no coincidences. However, we do stand amazed even still at what happened. We have tried to follow the path that He has put before us and tried not to get ahead of Him because that is when we would fail. Satan attacked us but we also found out this: Our God is more powerful.

The lessons learned from being a part of Amy For Africa will be with me forever. I have learned to have a more generous heart, be more active in reading the Bible, to reach out and help others whenever I could. A yearning to be part of something so great and so God inspired has literally left me speechless.

I thank God for allowing me to play even a small role in Amy For Africa and it is my prayer that this book will serve to inspire others to step out in faith and do something for Jesus Christ. After all, He did everything for us.

CHAPTER ONE
THRILLS AND CHILLS

On the morning of April 15, 2013, first-time Boston Marathon competitor Amy Compston, accompanied by her husband Chris, thirteen-year-old daughter Skylar, two-year-old son Jarek, father Steve Wesolowski, sister Amanda Evans and her niece Reagan Evans, caught an early subway ride to the finish line where everybody in the family but Amy would be perched for the day. It was Race Day and it wasn't even 6 a.m. yet.

There was a chill in the air with a temperature hovering between forty to forty-five degrees – perfect running weather. Some of the other runners had started to congregate near the finish line where a bus would soon whisk them away, exactly 26.2 miles away, at 7 a.m. Many were wearing hoodies, sweatpants and gloves to fight off some of the sharp chill although it later warmed up to fifty-four degrees.

There were three waves of runners, with about 10,000 participants in each wave, based on entry times. Amy's wave of runners would not start the Boston Marathon until around 10:30 a.m. But she had to catch the bus ride to Hopkinton where the marathon would begin. It is almost a straight line from Hopkinton to the finish line

CHAPTER ONE

on Boylston Street. Boston Marathon fans line both sides of the streets, sometimes five and six deep, from start to finish. They are emotional fans too, who cheer and encourage the competitors.

Chris, along with his father-in-law, Amy's sister Amanda and three children parked themselves at the finish line, being some of the first fans to arrive. Later in the day, nobody would be able to get near the spot the Compston family of twenty-one staked out. There was a nearby Starbucks that served as the perfect bathroom retreat, too. Eleven children of the twenty-one at the finish line paraded to that Starbucks bathroom most of the day for breaks. Of course, a few cups of Joe were purchased by the adults. The family wanted to be near the finish line to capture a Kodak moment of Amy and to photograph some of the Olympians in the race.

For about three hours, Amy's time was spent in the runner's village sizing up the competition while anxiously awaiting the start of the race. This wasn't like the other marathons, where she could easily find someone who didn't look like they belonged. "At other marathons, you go there and you see people who don't look like runners," she said. "Here everyone is very lean, very experienced runners. There was no one you could look at and say 'I got them.'"

The lesson: Only serious runners participate in the Boston Marathon. They are serious about running, runners who have trained and trained hard, just like she had. She was not intimidated by the other runners but understood this was going to be different. That difference showed right away when one of the runners came to her, almost like an angel.

"A lady asked if she could pray with me in the runner's village," Amy said. "I had never met her before. It was like God was reassuring me He was right there."

THRILLS AND CHILLS

Amy appreciated the affirmation that God was with her. She is a faith-based runner who spends eighty percent of her training in a conversation with God. Her faith had grown in ways she never fathomed since July, 2012, after she and her husband turned their lives completely over to God. Every day had become a little better than the last one.

Now, here she was, on one of the world's biggest athletic stages at the Boston Marathon. God had blessed her and she knew it. It was almost a pinch-me kind of moment. She was determined to do what she had trained to do — run her best and glorify God along the way. That was the plan anyway.

The Boston Marathon is unlike any other long distance race in the world. Organized by the Boston Athletic Association, this was the 117th edition of American's first and oldest marathon. They had invited 23,336 competitors, from all fifty states plus Washington D.C. and Puerto Rico, and from ninety-two countries.

Marathon weekend in Boston is like no other anywhere in the world with an estimated 500,000 visitors on hand. Those who live in and around Boston embrace the race as their very own. Huge banners hung from every light-post in town, proudly displaying the elite Americans running in the 2013 Boston Marathon. Runners wearing their Boston Marathon jackets are greeted like celebrities at every turn as they walk down the street or take a seat in a restaurant.

Since being accepted for the marathon six months prior, qualifying with her time in the Dayton Air Force Marathon, Amy studied and read everything she could about the Boston Marathon. She became engrossed in its history and its nuances. The more she read, the more she learned. She had an insatiable appetite for the Boston Marathon. She studied like it was her college final exam and she had

CHAPTER ONE

to record a perfect score.

Her family arrived in Boston on Thursday, four days before the race. They were there not only to celebrate Amy's participation in the marathon but also to take in the sights and sounds of the world's premier running event and this All-American city. None of it disappointed them. They went to a game at Fenway Park where the Red Sox won on Saturday afternoon, and Amanda and Chris competed in the Boston Marathon 5K early Sunday morning. They finished down the same path runners would follow a day later with the famous Citgo sign behind them. The town was buzzing with excitement and everybody could feel it.

At most marathons, the runner expos last only one day but at Boston the expo goes on for three days. They were able to meet several Olympians on Sunday and some of them even shared advice about the marathon.

"Ryan Hall said to start out slowly because the hills will tear up your legs," Amy said. "I'm going to listen to what he has to say. He holds the American record in Boston."

While sitting in the runner's village, wondering if 10:30 was ever going to arrive, Amy had her photograph taken in front of the Welcome to Hopkinton sign – a traditional picture that every runner looks forward to having as a keepsake. That's where the Boston Marathon starts, where this long straight line of 26.2 miles begins. She had heard about the infamous Newton hills, especially Heartbreak Hill, and wondered to herself how she would conquer it. It was never if with Amy, it was always how. She knew this was going to be a triumphant run. She had trained hard but she had prayed harder.

"They (the hills) weren't as bad as what I expected after running around here," she said.

THRILLS AND CHILLS

The hills of northeastern Kentucky, in the small town of Ashland, Kentucky, had its challenges, especially a half-mile nearly straight up stretch called Ashland Avenue only a few blocks from her home. That provided the perfect training ground for Boston's hilly terrain.

After twenty-six seconds of silence to honor the victims of the Sandy Hook Elementary School shooting, the marathon got under way with fifty-two wheelchair competitors leaving Hopkinton at 9:17 a.m. At 9:30 a.m., fifty-one elite women left the starting line, followed by the elite men and wave one at 10 a.m. The remaining competitors were released in two waves over the next forty minutes.

From the start of the marathon at Hopkinton, to the end of the race on Boylston Street, it was wall-to-wall people. They lined both sides of the street, cheering on runners as they passed. Some of them asked for kisses from the runners while the children looked for a hand slap as they jumped up and down with excitement. People are dressed in costumes and some of the same ones looking for a little kiss also had already had a little too much to drink. But everybody was cheering because in Boston, on this day, everybody really does know your name.

Fans give shout-outs to runners based on what they were wearing. Amy was wearing a shirt with Team 413 (based on Philipians 4:13) on it so they called her 413. The encouragement of the fans on the street cheering for the runners gives a needed boost, Amy said.

"It's like a tailgating party," she said. "I would slap kids' hands. But, uh, no kisses. That was more the Wellesley College girls who were asking for that."

There are no food stations along the route because fans supply runners with "any food you'd ever dream of having," Amy said.

CHAPTER ONE

"Fans lined on the streets from the start of the race to the finish was unlike anything I'd ever experienced. That's what gets you addicted to Boston ... you have to go back."

Runners mostly stay in the same pack where they started. "You're never by yourself but it's not congested," she said. "You're almost with the same people the whole time."

After running about twenty-five miles, Compston was beginning to hit the dreaded wall, when the body starts shutting down from depletion of all glucose. The finish line is on Boylston Street in front of the Boston Public Library, midway between Exeter and Dartmouth streets. Runners get their first glimpse of the finish after making a turn from Hereford Street onto Boylston. From there, the final three-and-a-half blocks, past Gloucester, Fairfield and Exeter streets is filled with thousands of screaming spectators.

"When I made it onto Boylston Street I hadn't seen my family," she said. "When I finally did see them it was so exciting. I waved, then I was like 'It's time to go!' I began to sprint because I wanted to finish strong."

Compston crossed the finish line and a feeling of exhilaration and exhaustion swept over her tired body. Her mind was racing as she bent over at the waist and looked back on an amazing spirit-filled journey with God. She had competed in the world's most prestigious long distance race in her third marathon, had done it in a personal best time of three hours, twenty-seven minutes and fifty-four seconds. It was a moment for her to treasure, to celebrate, to remember and cherish. But the day turned into horror almost in an instant.

Chris knew where he was supposed to meet with Amy in the family meeting area, about two blocks from the finish line. Runners are fenced away from the spectators after finishing and they are encouraged to stop at several stations set up along the way for a blanket, their medal, water and food.

"You're drained and wanting the food and water. You also want, most importantly, your Boston medal."

Amy had finished the race around 2:20 p.m. She was drained and exhausted. They called the family and told them to meet at the subway. "I told Chris I couldn't walk back to them," she said. Interestingly, when Amy had finished the race, she contemplated going back to the family since they were so close to the finish line, but decided to follow race protocol. It proved to be the right decision. "That was the Lord protecting us again," she said.

The remainder of the family – twenty in all minus Chris and Amy– left together to meet them at the subway station. They went down an alley because it seemed like a shortcut at the time. That turned out to be a fateful decision as well.

At 2:50 p.m., almost two hours after the winners had completed the race, two explosions occurred near the finish line where Amy's family had just been minutes before. Three spectators were killed and 265 others were injured. Among the injured, seventeen were in critical condition. At least fourteen required amputations. The race was halted eight minutes after the explosions and more than five thousand participants were unable to finish.

Chris and Amy still did not know the tragedy that had happened at the finish line.

"We were sitting on a bench waiting for them to get there when a lady asked if she could use our phone," Amy remembered. "We said 'Sure, here.' She asked us if we'd heard what happened. We said 'No' and she said 'There's been a bombing.' It was a moment of disbelief and shock."

CHAPTER ONE

Amy said she was already disoriented after running the marathon and the immediate concern was making sure all of the family members were safe and together again. They got the cell phone back and were able to make contact with the family and learned everyone was unharmed. The connection lasted only about five seconds before all phone service in the area was cut off.

"We tried to leave the subway (station) to find our family and the police told us to get on the subway and get out of the city," she said. "They (the family) went to a park somewhere in the city. They weren't allowed on the closest subway to them but eventually got on one. We were separated for an hour until we all got together again."

Amy and Chris heard reports of the second bomb while riding on the subway. It was all like a frightening nightmare.

The rest of the family was even separated from each other for a short time among the confusion. Eventually, they were able to get on a subway and return to where the family was staying three miles outside of town.

On the subway ride, tears were streaming down Amy's face as the realization of what had happened began to sink in. What was supposed to be a day of joy had turned into one of disaster. Her heart ached for those who were injured and for those who weren't allowed to finish the race after undergoing months and months of training. All she could think was "Why? Why would someone do this?"

She was hurting for those families who had lost loved ones and for those who were injured, but praised God that He chose to spare her family. There was no way to explain what had transpired since early that morning when she started running in the Boston Marathon.

THRILLS AND CHILLS

"I was crying on the way home," she said. "It's such an emotional day anyway. I couldn't believe I was at the Boston Marathon, and now I can't believe I was at the Boston Marathon where there was a terrorist attack."

When the family was finally together again, eleven children and eleven adults, not a word was spoken. "We hugged and we cried tears of joy because we were all safe but also tears of sadness for what just took place," Amy said. "The kids were silent. We turned the news on and watched. We couldn't believe we were part of that."

When reports showed where the two bombs were located, they realized how close the family had been the entire day. They were standing only a few feet away. "We were in pure shock. I could have been planning 21 funerals," she said, praising God that day for sparing her life and the life of her family.

Amy's faith that helped motivate her through the grueling marathon training was now helping her and her family cope with the horrific event. "I can just see how everything played out with God watching over," she said, crediting God with protecting all of them.

Amy's mother, Kathy Whitely, said it was a long day of waiting but also one of excitement. The children were diligent in passing out gospel tracts all day long while the rest of the family kept track of Amy's progress in the race with an App on their cell phones.

"We stood there and talked, had a good time together, waiting for Amy to come," Kathy said. "She starts coming down the street and we're all screaming and taking pictures. Everybody was so excited when she crossed that finish line."

She said they were able to speak with Amy on the cell phone and she told them they would have to meet her.

After gathering everybody together, Andy Wesolowski, Amy's

CHAPTER ONE

brother, pointed them in the direction they should be going, which was between two buildings down an alley.

"My son says 'Let's not go through this crowd. Let's go down this street and get away from the crowd where we can move faster.' We went down the alley, all 20 of us because Chris had already left to meet Amy. Somewhere along in there, I hear this explosion. I thought it was two rail cars hitting together. Living in eastern Kentucky that was a sound I was used to hearing. All of the sudden, I hear another explosion."

Her son-in-law, Mike Vazquez, said what everybody else was thinking: it sounded like a bomb. "Mike, Traci and I kind of looked at each other. None of us said a word," Kathy said.

They went on to the subway, only to find it closed, and that is where they learned it was a bomb. Kathy was concerned for everybody but she had heard from Chris and Amy and knew they were unharmed. Her attention turned to her father, Gerald Womack, who was home in Chicago.

"His whole family was here in Boston," she said. "I finally got through to him and said 'Dad, we're all OK. There's been a bomb.' I was rattling on to him. All he heard was 'We're OK, bomb.' Then he turned the news on and saw what was going on."

Eventually, the family was reunited where they were staying in Boston. They were shocked but safe and sound. Not a word had to be spoken by anyone for a message of love to be received. It was a time of mixed emotions, hugging, crying, rejoicing and worrying.

"It was a special time for all of us," Kathy said. "We just cried. Then we turned the TV on to see what happened. We couldn't believe it. I felt like the Lord protected us having to go down that street. We could have been very well right there where that bomb was. We were so thankful that God parted the Red Sea and showed us we need to go this way."

Almost immediately after arriving back together, Kathy said, the family took a photograph with everyone in it. It remains a treasured keepsake from the trip and a photograph that Amy uses when talking about the events of that day.

Amy's children asked questions about why the bombing happened, and she told them there is no explanation. "It's just evil, pure evil." Faith was also motivating the family to enjoy Boston as much as they could despite the attack. They were out the next day, taking in the sites.

"The city was open," Amy said. "They wanted things to go back to normal. There was a military presence, Army men with machine guns and grenades hanging off them. You were searched everywhere you went. But that made you feel safe. We went to Harvard, MIT, downtown Boston … we had a peace about it, that peace that God gives that passes all understanding. We even went to Cheers (restaurant and bar) that evening. We were refusing to be overcome by evil. We all have very strong faith, so we don't fear. Fear's from the devil. It's all God's will, whatever happens."

They went with Christian tracts in hand to Boston and there were many more people willing to receive them than the previous day before the bombs had shaken the world.

Amy at the Boston Marathon in April 2013.

Amy holds her Boston Marathon medal.

The front page of The Independent in Ashland, Ky., after the Boston Marathon bombings.

Amy at the starting point in Boston.

Amy with her family in Boston, one hour after the bombing.

Amy and husband Chris Compston outside Fenway Park in April 2013.

Amy and her father, Steve Wesolowsk, in Boston before the 2013 Boston Marathon.

CHAPTER TWO
RUNNING IN THE WRONG DIRECTION

When Amy was growing up, she was in a Christian home in Greenup County as the youngest of four siblings. She had two older sisters, Traci and Amanda, and a big brother in Andy. There is two years age difference between each child.

Her mother played piano for the church and her father was the church treasurer. The family was in church when the doors were open - every Sunday morning, Sunday night and Wednesday night. Amy remembers her mother reading her Bible every morning, an example she would later follow.

Steve, her father, was in law enforcement in Greenup County, Kentucky, and Kathy, her mother, was mostly a stay-at-home mom. Amy said her parents were "pretty strict when it came to religion and church." The girls were allowed to wear only skirts, no pants ever, until the family moved to Chicago when Amy was five. The winters were so brutally cold in Chicago, Steve and Kathy allowed the girls to start wearing pants. The family later moved back to Greenup County and the new dress code came with them.

CHAPTER TWO

Amy was a mommy's girl when she was a baby, her mother remembered. "She would tuck her arms in when I was holding her. She didn't want everybody else to talk to her and if anybody told her she was beautiful, she really didn't like that. She'd get so angry. I think that changed when she got a little older."

Little Amy had a little spirit in her though, her father said. "Amy, when she was growing up, she was a tough one. You didn't want to get in her way in the mornings, that's for sure."

She was closest to her brother, Andy, who is two years older. They were pre-school playmates most days and Amy remembers playing "Mike and Jim" with Andy.

"Everybody thought they were twins," Kathy said. "One was blonde and the other was brown-headed. When they started going to school, they split up a little bit and made other friends. But they've always been very close."

School was never difficult for Amy, her mother said. "I don't think she ever brought homework home. She was very intelligent and always made great grades. She liked sports, running mostly, but she played soccer too. I actually liked soccer better because I could see her do something the whole time. In track you waited all day long for her to run a little distance."

Amy began running when she was eleven and a sixth-grader at Wurtland Middle School when a friend, Jenna Marshall, asked her to join the high school track team. They didn't have middle school track in Greenup County schools at the time so anyone who wanted to run had to compete on the high school level. Amy learned rather quickly that this running was something she did well. "I could easily crank out a six-minute mile and I was winning first, second and third place in almost all the local competitions. I had found something I

RUNNING IN THE WRONG DIRECTION

was good at and I loved it."

She loved it so much that she began getting up at 5 a.m. before school just to go run. She ran before school and after school, sometimes six miles a day. She ran for the fun of it and a passion was being developed in her life.

"She did start running at an early age," Amanda said. "I remember her running up and down the road. I would ask myself, 'Why is she running up and down the road?' She would go out and run. That was Amy."

Amy also ran out of frustration when she was angry or trying to deal with situations at home, be it a fight with her parents or a disagreement with a sibling. It was a way for her to get away from everything and process it. "Running was definitely therapeutic," she said. "I started running in, say March, when I was eleven. My parents got divorced in August that same year. Anytime I was mad or angry or downright out of control, I would take off and go run to deal with it so I wouldn't blow up on them."

When Amy's parents divorced, the family model changed drastically. Her mother found herself needing a job and, at the urging of a friend, enrolled in college. That time away took a toll on the family with the children often having to fend for themselves.

"That's when Amy started getting into a lot of situations that caused her a lot of difficulty in the future because I wasn't there," her mother said. "I was in school, then tutoring at school. I did a lot of work at school as a teacher's aide that I got paid for. But then I wasn't home. The children suffered when I was not there. Not just Amy, all of them."

Amy says now she understands better how that did impact her. "I didn't realize it until I was an adult. At that time, my dad moved

CHAPTER TWO

out and I didn't have a strong father figure there. My mom had to get a job and go back to school. That left my eighteen-year-old sister (Amanda), whenever she was there, taking care of us. They left me and Andy home a lot. Without proper guidance, a kid is going to do what a kid is going to do. I was twelve years old and hanging out with the wrong crowd."

Amy said one memory she had with Amanda was when her sister was babysitting the others. "She would not let us watch 'Days of Our Lives' until we did our chores. Amanda was always in control, or tried to be."

The time alone wasn't always put to the best use, especially by Amy. Meanwhile, she was looking up to her sister Amanda, who was six years older and enjoying a reckless lifestyle herself.

"She was just fun to me," Amy said. "Everything she did looked so fun and exciting. She was getting in the party crowd herself, which is what most eighteen-year-olds do. It looked fun and she let me be a part of it. It was at my second party I met this guy who I thought was God's gift to me. I met him in eighth grade and he wouldn't date me until I was in high school. But I hung around the party scene because of him. Amanda hung out with his brother and we all hung out together."

Amy was drinking alcohol at the age of twelve, even getting drunk once at her house on New Year's Eve. "The first time I drank alcohol I was twelve," Amy said. "It was at my mom's house, a small New Year's Eve party. I remember telling a friend at school 'I got drunk last night.' I was in band class. A few months later, Amanda had a huge party at my mom's house, like 300 people. It was crazy. Drugs were everywhere in the basement. I got so drunk. I remember Dad coming there with his police friends. They gave me a breathalyzer and I blew a 4.0. Dad had found me passed out lying in my own urine." Parties and an unsavory lifestyle would follow Amy for the next sixteen years of her life.

Her sister, Amanda, remembers those parties and her disregard for her little sister. "She was drinking and I remember my sister Traci saying 'Amy's drinking!' I was like, 'Well, don't worry about it.' I was being so self-absorbed with myself."

But that night the party was out of control and the local authorities were called to the house. Steve Wesolowski was part of the Greenup County Sheriff Department entourage that came to his old home and sorted out the problems. The first person he confronted after seeing his passed out twelve-year-old daughter, Amy, was her sister Amanda. He wanted answers.

"I was completely drunk and I remember him coming into the room and saying 'Look at what you have done to your sister!' It was very overwhelming at the time and even more so after I sobered up and saw what I had allowed to happen," Amanda said. "She's looking up to me and I'm drinking and using drugs. She thought that was the way to have fun. I don't know if she really looked up to me but she did follow in that footpath."

That first party, which resulted in Amy getting drunk for the first time, is something that still haunts Amanda.

"So many things were going on in that house (that night) that was hard for anybody to handle, let alone a twelve-year-old. But I had no regard for it, I didn't care. I thought it was fine (that Amy was drinking)," she said. "We were having the parties and I didn't think anything about her being there. I don't know if it was because I felt so close to Amy. Even though she was twelve, we had grown up together. To me she was just my sister. I wasn't thinking she was

CHAPTER TWO

twelve years old. The thing I look back the most on is that very first party. I remember my dad being so disappointed because I allowed this to happen to my baby sister."

In her testimony, Amy talks about falling for the "senior football player" at the age of fourteen when she was a freshman in school and how he introduced her to a partying lifestyle of premarital sex, alcohol and drugs. By the age of fourteen, she already had boys sleeping over. She had started on a dangerous path at a young age.

At first, it was mostly marijuana and alcohol that were her vices but that quickly progressed into prescription pills and even worse later in life when she "couldn't get high enough" with marijuana and alcohol. She dabbled in heroin, cocaine, crystal meth, Ecstasy, and acid. However, Amy was conscious enough of what she was doing that if the drug did things she didn't like to her, she didn't make them a habit. She is fortunate the addictions weren't as severe with her as they can be with others.

During her one and only experience with acid, she and several other girlfriends, riding in the backseat of a car, thought they saw a giant elf bounding around in Wurtland, Kentucky, where they were being driven around by some boys. "That was my one and only experience with acid," she said. "I never took it again."

However, marijuana was a habit. She said there were not many days between the age of 15 and 28 that she didn't smoke at least one joint and usually it was a lot more. Except for when she was pregnant with her children, it wasn't unusual for Amy to be lighting up at anytime, day or night.

"Once I got in high school it was every weekend," she said. "Me and that guy got together. It went from every weekend to every day. But I always got my run in. I think that's what started me getting

RUNNING IN THE WRONG DIRECTION

up so early to run. I knew if I didn't do it then I'd be too stoned to do it later."

Her mother, trying to juggle multiple jobs, did not know the extent of her daughter's problems until she overdosed at the age of fifteen.

Even though Amy knew it was wrong and knew what it may do to her body, she was never above experimenting with drugs. Even at the age of fifteen, she wanted to fit in with the other girls in her circle of friends and ingested thirty Xanax pills in one hour, snorting some and taking some by mouth. She found herself in the Intensive Care Unit at Our Lady of Bellefonte Hospital with tubes in every orifice of her body and a heart rate of only 29. Normal heart rates are between 60 and 100 so Amy's heart rate had nurses concerned.

However, her mother told the nurses that Amy's heart rate was going to be OK, that she was a runner and runners have lower heart rates. Her mother also asked God to spare her daughter, that she knew He had plans for her. Amy said her praying mother made a difference that night and many others during a time when Amy's life was anything but Christian.

"Mom did try," Amy said. "She only thinks the best of anyone. As well as I remember, we didn't let Dad know. Mom had custody of us. There was a lot of stuff we didn't tell Dad. I don't even know if he knew about the overdoses. Mom didn't want him taking me away from her."

Amy's goal in life had become to find a way to get accepted and find a way to get high. It didn't matter to her how either happened. She was looking for fulfillment from friends and from drugs but never found it. That didn't keep her from trying over and over again.

It was after the first overdose that Amy's life as a competitive

CHAPTER TWO

runner came to a close, at least as a high school runner. She was only fifteen and a sophomore but the stigma of being someone who overdosed was too much socially for her to handle. She was lumped with the drug crowd, at least in her own mind, from the way the other students looked at her.

"I felt so embarrassed and looked down upon. My soccer coach was so humiliated by me, so disappointed, and rightfully so. But, as a fifteen-year-old, I got very defensive. I was like 'Whatever! Get over yourself!' I was going to do what I wanted to do. I was kind of in rebellion and quit soccer and quit running track. It really affected me when I overdosed and everybody (at school) knew about it. It threw me into that crowd. I was accepted with those people. The good kids, if you want to call them that, didn't want to have anything to do with me, or at least that's what I thought."

But her other "drug friends" encouraged Amy to continue experimenting in the wrong direction like they were doing and she did. Peer pressure, combined with some mistakes made, proved to be a cocktail that would keep her in a downward path that had no soft landing.

Six months after overdosing on Xanax, Amy and three other girls "got ready for the school dance" by drinking a fifth of whiskey after dropping Xanax and Percocets into it. They drank the entire bottle in ninety minutes and then went stumbling to the dance. Someone saw them and knew the girls were in trouble so they called the police. "I don't know who that was to this day but I praise God for them," she said. "These days people aren't courageous enough to do anything. They don't want to get involved. I'm so glad whoever this was did say something, because it may have saved my life."

When the officers arrived they immediately called for an am-

RUNNING IN THE WRONG DIRECTION

bulance to take the girls to the emergency room. Her mother again met Amy in the ER and prayed over her all night. She prayed over how she was supposed to handle this as a mother since none of her other children had gone to this extreme in this type of destructive lifestyle.

They sent in psychologists and others to speak with Amy and they asked her if she was suicidal. "I told them 'No, I'm just trying to get high.' I was honest with them," she said. "The doctors took that answer. That was good enough for them."

Amy's mom didn't think there was anything psychological wrong but she did know something was missing in her daughter's life - and it was Jesus Christ. With that, she enrolled her in Christian drug counseling at Bridges Christian Church. They went every Friday and Amy's counselor talked to her about Jesus, His love, and about how she needed Him. Amy listened and she knows now that some of it stuck inside her heart because "God's Word does not return void." But mostly, at least at the time, she hated the Christian drug counseling and did it only to stay on her mother's good side. "If I went to Christian drug counseling, I could go to the game on Friday night," she said. "That was a good enough trade for me. I went to drug counseling high sometimes and mom didn't know it. I hated every second of it but I know some of what they were teaching me stuck in my heart."

Her mother said the church had helped her with divorce counseling and she didn't know where else to turn. They went every Friday for nine months.

"I think I grew more out of that experience than she did at the time. But God was still planting those seeds in her heart. To me, I thought everything was OK and then I find out differently as time went on."

Amanda, who had moved to Chicago when Amy was 13,

CHAPTER TWO

learned of the downhill spiral and wanted to help. "I left the house when I was nineteen," said Amanda. "I got to introduce Amy to the partying lifestyle and then I left. I was gone a few years when things really got out of control. Amy overdosed the second time and they didn't think she was going to make it. Mom called and I said 'I'm going to move back,' as if I could help the situation in any way. When I got back home we continued to do drugs together and drinking."

At the age of seventeen, Amy's life was still spinning completely away from anything God-centered. But the one thing she remained good at was running. She had stopped competing at the age of fifteen but continued to run nearly on a daily basis. It was something she craved even more than the marijuana, alcohol and drugs.

One night after partying through the night with friends, she woke up early and went to the gym to work out. "Because I've always been a runner," she said. On the way home after her workout though, she barreled into the back of a pickup truck while going 40 miles per hour. The driver of the pickup and his two young sons walked away from the accident without injury.

"I praise God for that today," she said.

But Amy wasn't as lucky. Her head slammed into the steering wheel, causing a traumatic facial injury on her forehead. The force of the seat belt trying to hold her in snapped her collarbone. She was back at OLBH where they stabilized her injuries and then called in a plastic surgeon to sew up the damage. He worked on her face for six hours, putting in more than three hundred fifty stitches, sewing her eyelids back together, her nerves back together and giving her a facelift, which included a Botox treatment.

"But do you know what? God's hand of mercy was on me that day, too," she said. "I walked out of that hospital that same night.

RUNNING IN THE WRONG DIRECTION

There was no brain bleed, I wasn't paralyzed, and there was no brain damage. It was clearly God protecting me."

When she arrived at the ER, they wanted a urine sample for a drug test.

"I was so freaked out. I ended up not peeing … praise the Lord! They did a blood-alcohol level and it came back fine. I think God was sparing her (Amy's mother) from that. I don't think she could have handled it. How did it come back clean? I don't know but thank you Lord!"

Her mother, who is now in the medical field, was not at the time of the accident. But she asked to watch as the doctor worked on her daughter. She had to step away a couple of times after feeling "a warm sensation." Kathy praises God not only for Amy's recovery but also that he led her to a friend who said she needed to ask for a plastic surgeon.

"He stood there for six hours and sewed her face together and it was a blessing," Kathy said. "She had just gotten a tongue ring about a week before. They had to take it out before surgery. He asked her 'Do you want this back in?' and she said 'No, just leave it out.' I think she was probably happy she did that, too."

Amy's time of healing was also a time of bonding with her mother. They both slept in the living room – Amy in an easy chair and her mother next to her. But it wasn't long until Amy was returning to the only lifestyle she really ever knew or at least the one where she found the most happiness and feeling of being accepted.

"It had such a grip on me," she said of the drugs and alcohol. "I couldn't get out. I didn't feel accepted anywhere except in the lifestyle."

The Wesolowski children were always
ready to make you smile.

Only two years separates Amy and Andy, who were inseparable playmates when they were young.

Andy and Amy played many games together, including being "Mike and Jim."

Steve and Kathy Wesolowski and the family:
Traci and Amanda (middle row) and Amy
and Andy (bottom row).

Daddy Steve Wesolowski and Amy.

Sisters Amy and Amanda were always
the best of friends.

CHAPTER THREE
'YOU CAN'T GET HIGH ENOUGH'

Somehow, despite living like the devil, Amy managed to graduate from Greenup County High School. But she remained in the wrong circle of friends, friends who looked for nothing more than their next high and they didn't mind trying anything to get it. She had smoked marijuana on a daily basis from the age of fourteen but a joint and a drink didn't give her the same punch it once did.

"When you get in that lifestyle, you can't get high enough. You want to experience the same kind of high you had the first time. So you have to go harder. That's when I started experimenting with the harder drugs like heroin, cocaine, crystal meth, acid and Ecstasy. I was looking for fulfillment, contentment, anything, to make me feel that high again. I was looking in all the wrong places and hanging out with all the wrong people. I know now the only way you can get that fulfillment, that acceptance, is in Jesus Christ. That's the only way."

Amy remembers on graduation night staying up the entire night doing crystal meth. "I wanted acceptance, to belong to some-

CHAPTER THREE

thing. The lifestyle continued and even got worse when I got older."

From the time she was eighteen, Amy's routine was smoking joints every day and living for the weekend. She went to the bars in Ironton, Ohio, and Huntington, West Virginia, every Thursday, Friday and Saturday. Oftentimes she went to church on Sunday still smelling of alcohol.

"As this is going on, I'm still going to church, working, and I'm in nursing school," she said.

She worked part-time jobs at several places and she saved her money for the weekend. "I'd get paid on Fridays, take out the money I needed to pay my bills, and the rest went to the bars. That's what I did every weekend from the time I was eighteen until twenty when I got pregnant with my first son. When I look back on it now, it was disgusting. There was some happiness for a few moments but it was mostly nastiness and disgust the next morning. I wasn't content, I wasn't happy, but it's all I knew. I couldn't get away from it. Satan had his stronghold on me and I couldn't break it."

Her lifestyle continued to be one of reckless abandon. She smoked joints every day, partied on the weekends and continued to live like the devil. Amy actually first met her husband-to-be, Chris Compston, in Shenanigan's in Ironton. "I don't remember it but Amanda says that's where she introduced us for the first time."

Amy and Chris had a definite attraction to each other and they "dated" for about three months after meeting. But the dates were nothing more than late evenings in the bar drinking and then sleeping with each other that night. Chris, who was going through a divorce, had his own problems beyond reckless drinking. He also had a family, two little girls, Skylar and Bailee, to deal with in his life. Amy was only 18 at the time and wanted nothing to do with a ready-made

'YOU CAN'T GET HIGH ENOUGH'

family. She was far from ready to settle down to a family lifestyle of any kind so the two of them eventually went their separate ways. "I told him, 'You have a family and you need to take care of them. Go do that. You need to do that.' I didn't want that in my life then," she said. "He was crying, saying he loved me. I said, 'No, go take care of your family.'"

There are many nights during Amy's bar days that she doesn't remember anything that happened. One night, she and a girlfriend woke up in an abandoned warehouse in Ashland and had no idea how they had gotten there. The night had started out in Ironton, in a bar, with too many drinks. That lifestyle was defining Amy but she would not stay sober enough to listen to anybody.

But she still ran. Every day she ran. It was the only real release she had from a life that she wasn't happy living. But Satan wasn't happy that he hadn't taken away her joy for running, a gift that God had given her to use for Him. Satan began feeding her lies about being too fat and Amy began starving herself.

"I would eat one baked potato all day and run five and six miles. I would make myself vomit eight and nine times a night. I thought if I were skinnier, maybe he would like me or she would be my friend. Satan was telling me these lies and I believed him. He is the father of lies and he'll do anything to destroy your gift that God has given you. He didn't want me running. You can't run marathons if you're starving yourself to death."

Through it all, Amy began attending nursing school at Ashland Community Technical College. One of her classmates was her mother, who had been laid off from American Electric Power. As a result of the layoff, though, came an offer to pay for college for her and Amy. They were accepted to nursing class together, took the

CHAPTER THREE

same classes and clinical groups together and became friends along with being mother and daughter. It was during that time, when Amy was between seventeen and twenty years old, that they really drew close.

"My mom then became my best friend," Amy said. "Even with all the partying, drugs and alcohol … studying came first. Then I would stay up all night. I took a lot of Stackers to get me through it all. Those were speed pills you could buy at the gas station. That's also when I fell in love with coffee."

When the first test came back from nursing classes, mother knew best and Amy's competitive side came out.

"When she got a higher score than me, I was like 'OK, it's on.'" Probably without the friendly competition with her mother, she may not have made it through nursing school. But even during the time she was taking classes, her sinful life was in full swing during the weekends.

"We rode together every day, were in the same clinical groups and me and my mom grew very close," Amy said. "She was my best friend. I lived with her still; lived in her basement. Mom kind of knew what was going on. Mom always loved me. It was the one place where I could see Jesus's love in my life. She never rejected me, never told me to get out. She showed tough love sometimes but always loved me no matter how disgusting my lifestyle."

Kathy loved her daughter like mothers do. She didn't approve of the lifestyle but "there was not a lot I could do about it. I knew she was smoking marijuana but I didn't know how it was leading to other things too. I had to release her to the Lord. I encouraged her, told her how God spared you from this and from that so he must have something for you to do. I don't know how to fix this situation. You

'YOU CAN'T GET HIGH ENOUGH'

just pray through them."

Amy became pregnant at the age of twenty and she said the partying and poor eating habits stopped for those nine months. "But as soon as I could get back to it, I did." She had a son, Elias Jackson, later to be called "Bear," so now her responsibility had taken on a new twist. Bear was the best thing that came of the relationship between Amy and Bear's father, Seth Jackson. They lived together while she was pregnant but had a strained relationship. Amy left him when Bear was five-and-a-half months old.

"I didn't want to raise my baby in all the fighting," she said. Even though Amy and Seth were not happy together, Bear was a happy baby who was always smiling. He received his nickname at three months old because he was a big baby – not fat, but long. "I loved to hold him and cuddle with him. I always said he was my big Teddy Bear, which resulted in the nickname Bear."

"Even though I quickly returned to smoking pot after he was born, I always made sure he was in church. I knew it was vital."

Amy and Seth have a good relationship today and always want what is best for Bear. Seth has his son every Friday and Saturday.

"I named Bear, Elias Seth Jackson, after his dad. We did have some really good times but the bad outweighed the good," Amy said. "It was simply not God's plan for our lives to be together. But we did get the most amazing blessing from the relationship … Bear!"

Her mother made Amy promise not to marry Seth for at least six months after Bear was born, to let her hormones settle back to normal so she would not make an emotional decision. Amy said she would wait and then decided the relationship wasn't going to work.

"I knew Amy wasn't the same person she was when she met this fella," Kathy said.

CHAPTER THREE

It was Amy's good friend, the late Joe Stevens, who introduced her to Seth. They were both in nursing school – Seth in his first year and Amy in her second.

"My mistake, which really wasn't fair to Seth then, he didn't know I was in the drug scene and loved the bars. I pretended to be somebody else. I played the good role for a few months. We were together less than a year when I got pregnant with Bear. We stayed together, were going to get married, but that didn't work out."

Right before she became pregnant, she hired on at King's Daughters Medical Center.

She did find love though eventually with Chris Compston, who she had not seen for four years. But a lot had changed in that time. Chris was now divorced after the rocky marriage and was not living a Christian lifestyle either. Amy was a mother and was much more understanding of Chris's situation with his two daughters.

They may have never found each other if not for Amanda, who worked with Chris. She had a photograph of Amy on her desk. Amanda remembered the rest of the story: "He said, 'Who is that?' I said, 'That's my sister. Dude, I can't even introduce you. She's going to eat you up and spit you out. This will never work." Amy and Amanda were together in the bar when Chris arrived. "I told Amy, 'That's the guy who wanted to see you.' Amy was like, 'Why didn't you think I would like him? He's hot!' I didn't think it would work but they hit it off. They loved each other from the moment they saw each other."

However, it wasn't all roses and, as so often happens, life got in the way and Chris and Amy stopped dating. "They didn't see each other for a few years," Amanda said. "She had gotten with Seth and they had Bear." After that relationship came apart, Amy and Chris

'YOU CAN'T GET HIGH ENOUGH'

happened to run into each other again. Amanda recalls the day.

"They saw each other at the mall and Amy said, 'There's Chris Compston!' I was like, 'Really Amy?' But she was insistent on talking to him again. It was Amy's birthday weekend. I called Chris and asked if he wanted to meet us at Ruby Tuesday's. He said he wasn't sure but would try. He worked it out, came that night, and ever since they have been together and it still blows my mind to this day. I never thought she would have anything to do with Chris Compston."

When Chris and Amy first started dating for the second time in September 2006, Amy had her son, Bear, and Chris's daughters visited on weekends. Chris started working in the emergency room at King's Daughters as a scribe in 2007.

Their relationship progressed and they married on May 20, 2008, with a ceremony in Hawaii, a gift from a physician friend. It was a ceremony with only Chris, Amy, a woman preacher and a photographer.

Amy became pregnant with Jarek in 2010, about the same time that Chris was laid off from KDMC. Amy convinced him to enroll in school.

"It was amazing how God worked all that out," Amy said. "Chris got unemployment and God opened up the opportunity for all of his schooling to be paid for."

After receiving his LPN he was hired back by the hospital where he works today.

The family that started out with three – Chris, Amy and Bear – and weekend visits from Chris's daughters, was going to grow in a hurry. Chris was granted full custody of his daughters after a court battle, and Jarek's birth made six. Chris and Amy had a "yours, mine and ours" family situation.

CHAPTER THREE

Chris Compston grew up in Coal Grove, Ohio, and was an outstanding high school athlete. He was a good enough hurdler that he went to Rio Grande on a scholarship but only stayed for a year and moved back home. He says life with Amy was a "meant-to-be story."

Chris said the brief relationship with Amy when she was eighteen was mostly partying and drinking but the second time around, after she turned twenty-two and had a baby, things were different although not exactly the lifestyle where they needed to be.

"Drinking was something we did a lot especially on the weekends or when she wasn't working. The party scene wasn't quite as bad. On Sundays we'd get up and go to church. I was always in church, grew up in church but never took it serious. We were going through the motions. I know I went just to appease Amy because she wanted me to go."

Chris knew this much: He would do anything for this girl – even go to church. He found out rather quickly about her competitive streak. "She is absolutely competitive in everything, almost to a fault. That's why God put us together. I'm very laid-back and let things go by. Amy, from the moment I met her, she always had to be right. Her way was the right way. I liked that about her. It's one of the reasons I fell in love with her. Her brother even tried to warm me. 'Run! Get away now because she is crazy!' he told me."

Chris was a runner, too. When Amy told him she ran and invited him to go with her, he thought it was going to be easy. "I thought I'd blow her out of the water."

Of course, that did not happen. Chris was finding out quickly about Amy's passion for running. He loved that competitive side of her, the same kind of drive that he found out later would fuel her spiritually too.

'YOU CAN'T GET HIGH ENOUGH'

Even with a new family dynamic and more responsibility as an adult, Amy smoked pot every day and normally multiple times in a day. Alcohol was also part of the lifestyle for both of them. She said they did drugs in the bedroom with the door closed, ignoring the children's wishes on the other side. "We thought the kids didn't know what was going on, but they knew," she said. "They were asking us what we were going to have for supper or ask what we were doing in there. It's disgusting when I think back on it now."

Since God could not reach Amy mentally during the day because of the almost constant drug abuse, He found another way. "I was quenching the spirit during the day by filling my body with drugs and alcohol," she said. "God decided if I wasn't going to listen during the day, then He'd send me nightmares while I slept – and I knew it was Him. I'd have nightmares about losing my husband, nightmares about losing my children, nightmares about losing my career. I'd have them every night. He wasn't going to let me rest. If you are truly saved, God will not let you live comfortably in a lifestyle that is not pleasing to him. This was not His plan for my life."

She tried to brush the nightmares aside, but God was working on her. He directed her family to Unity Baptist Church in Ashland in the spring of 2012.

Amy's high school graduation night from Greenup County. She spent most of the evening high on crystal meth.

Amy and her sister, Amanda, at an Aerosmith concert where they were high on cocaine. It was during the time Amy was in college.

Amy and her mother, Kathy Whitely, who graduated nursing school together.

Chris and Amy two months into their relationship the second time around. Bear was 8 month old.

Chris and Amy on their wedding day in Hawaii.

CHAPTER FOUR
CONNECTING AS DISCIPLES

It was nine months before the Boston Marathon that Amy and Chris had a transformation in their Christian lives. They had joined a MasterLife class taught by Dr. Floyd Paris at Unity Baptist Church and it was life-changing. Even as they joined the MasterLife class in July of 2012, their lives were anything but Christian. They lived a life of lies. They wore several masks in life, including one for church, one for work, even one for the drug dealer, but they were doing anything but truly living for Christ.

Both of them were slaves to alcohol and drugs, an addiction that had been with Amy for more than half of her young life. She knew it was wrong and was disgusted by the decisions she had chosen but Satan had a stronghold on her life. Amy's outlet came only through running. That's when she could clear her head, that's when she could make a decision without Satan's influence. It was her sanctuary. But Satan's grip was mighty and strong. We underestimate his everyday power over us if we allow him inside our life. He had her right where he wanted her.

CHAPTER FOUR

Amy said she was saved at the age of nine when she attended a revival with her family. John Powell was the preacher and she came home that night and told her father that she needed Jesus and that she needed to be saved. They knelt by his bed and she asked Jesus into her heart. But that was it. Her growth as a born again Christian stopped right there. She remained an infant Christian until taking that MasterLife class nearly twenty years later.

"I was a baby Christian and, you know, babies can't do anything for themselves," she said. Amy didn't grow or mature as a Christian and, while saved through the blood of Jesus Christ, wasn't living for Him. She completely put Him aside in her life. She had no regard for His position in her life or anybody's life for that matter. God truly didn't matter.

How many have done that same thing? Churches often fail in teaching Christians how to be disciples. When a person is saved, it is not the end but the beginning. Without proper guidance, that decision to follow Jesus can quickly grow cold and old. While becoming a Christian is simple – simply believe and ask Jesus into your heart – growing into a mature Christian takes effort and study. It takes getting into God's Holy Word on a daily basis. It is Life's Answer Book. Just like an infant baby needs help to grow bigger and stronger, so do infant Christians. Amy remained that "baby" Christian for most of her growing up years. If you don't move toward God, you move away from Him. That's what happened to Amy. She began looking to the world, instead of The Word. She was looking for answers, for happiness, and for acceptance in places where it was not going to be found. Her addiction to drugs and alcohol came through during that searching. She knows now that she was looking in the wrong place.

CONNECTING AS DISCIPLES

It was during the MasterLife class though that Amy realized she was not living for Christ and not being obedient to His teachings. She asked herself: "Do I even love God?" Amy always said and even thought she loved God but God's Word, in John 14:23, says "If anyone loves me, he will obey my teachings." Amy was not obeying God at all. So did she really love Him? The more she learned, the more this infant Christian began to grow and develop. She also learned of the power of the Holy Spirit which before she thought "was only my seal for going to heaven." Brother Paris nurtured the MasterLife group and taught them about how the Holy Spirit lives in every saved person's life, and the power that came with that was stronger than anything this world has to offer. He taught them to call on that power that's inside each and every one of them if they are true believers of Jesus Christ.

"It's the power of the King of Kings, the Lord of Lords, the everlasting Father, the same power that raised Jesus Christ from the dead," Amy said. "That power is inside of me!!" When she realized that, it opened her eyes to a whole new world.

She had tried to stop drugs on her own many times, she had gone to counselors and organizations which had resources to help bring addictions to an end, but she always reverted back to that sin-filled lifestyle. Satan would fill her head with lies about how she was an addict, how she needed this lifestyle and how she couldn't stop. So why even try? You know you'll always come back, he would tell her. And she believed Satan's lies. "I couldn't beat those addictions – I'd tried to stop five hundred times – but the Holy Spirit could (beat them). When I tapped into that power, man, that was it. The addictions were over. It was done. When Brother Floyd taught me that, it changed my life. I had that power inside of me, living in me and I

CHAPTER FOUR

could call on it at any time."

Amy said she had no idea what she was signing up for at the time but she understands now it was no accident. The same held true for the rest of the class, she said.

"God put us together like an amazing puzzle. We all have similar stories. We'd tell Pastor Floyd the most insane things about ourselves and nothing shocked him. He just loved us and accepted what we said and took it back to the Bible. God loves us anyway no matter what we were doing. He taught us how to be true disciples of Jesus Christ. If you love me, you'll obey me. That hit me hard."

Chris and Amy and their family took a beach vacation and took along the MasterLife workbooks – along with some wine. But the transformation was taking place slowly but surely as they looked over the material on a daily basis.

"As I was reading those books and still drinking, I had to ask, 'Do I even love God?' It changed my life. That week is when I decided I can't do this anymore," Amy said.

Amy got serious with Christ. She took it so seriously, in fact, that she was willing to make a statement to her husband about the lifestyle they were in, a lifestyle that included doing drugs in the bedroom with the door shut while their children played in the next room. It was a reckless lifestyle that had to end and Amy was willing to do whatever was necessary to end it, even if it meant leaving the love of her life, Chris Compston. She took her son, "Bear," and went to her mother's house. She called Chris and told him she was done with the lifestyle, that she was tired of living four and five different lives. She was going to live one life and it was for Christ.

"My church friends knew Church Amy, my work friends knew Work Amy and my drug dealer knew Drug Amy," she said. "I didn't know who I was and I couldn't do it anymore. I said, 'God, I've made a mess of my life. Please, take it and do whatever you want with it. I don't care. Just take it.'"

If Chris wanted to join her, then good, but if not, they were done. It didn't take long for Chris to call back and tell her he was on board. He was taking the MasterLife class too and, along with Amy, God was working on him. He told Amy he was ready for a new life, that he was tired of the lifestyle that was not pleasing to God. They decided, as a couple, to turn over that lifestyle to God and start living for Him. Life suddenly took a 180 degree turn. They both put down the drugs and alcohol and gave God not only their problems, but their lives.

Since that time, Amy and Chris have been a couple on fire for God. Watching them grow as Christians has been an exhilarating experience for anybody paying attention. The lifestyle that had them trapped for so long was not there anymore. They had found a replacement for it, a spiritual replacement. The urge to light up a joint or go to the bars had disappeared from their lives. It's no longer even a consideration.

Amy credits her recovery to learning how the Holy Spirit, who lives within each person who has accepted Jesus as their Savior, can be unleashed for good. The power of the Holy Spirit is truly an amazing weapon that Christians have at their disposal, but sadly never unleash to the full extent of its power. It is literally God living inside us. Yet, for whatever reasons, we like to keep it tucked away and out of sight. We want to do it on our own. But as Christians, we have that power of the Holy Spirit living inside us! It's a power that defeats any addiction or any problem that's not of God.

Anybody that knew Chris and Amy would marvel at the trans-

CHAPTER FOUR

formation. They are now examples of God's amazing saving grace and how He can change anybody's life and use it for greatness for the Kingdom. They want to be used by God, in whatever way, big or small. They are still growing Christians but are no longer the "infants" that they were two years ago. They are new creatures in Christ and give Him all the praise and glory for every good thing in their lives.

Everybody from that MasterLife class – Chris and Amy, Amanda Evans and Samantha Caudill – became stronger Christians with a better idea of who they were serving and why they were serving Him. The teaching was sound, the study strong and the results simply astounding. It was a turnaround that frankly none of them expected when they signed up for the course.

"I never felt worthy of taking a class called MasterLife," Amy said. "I made Chris and Amanda join with me and I'm sure glad I did. It made a difference in their lives, too. Praise the Lord!"

Amanda wasn't sure about the class but reluctantly joined anyway at the insistence of her sister. "I started the group and, I'll be very honest, I was very hesitant to open up," she said. "I did not understand why I was there. I thought 'This is going to be a waste of time.' Amy and Chris were on board. They were saying it was going to be good for us, we're going to learn something."

Eventually, Amanda said, the program started changing her, too. "It was probably a few months before I started seeing a change. At first I'd read the book but didn't fill out the end, where there was a devotional time and you wrote down what you'd learned. The more I did that, the more I understood how becoming a disciple for Christ was important. It opened my eyes. Now I wouldn't change it for the world. I love those people. It did something as a group for us. It

CONNECTING AS DISCIPLES

changed us. Even though I was so hesitant and questioning 'Why am I doing this?' Amy saw I needed it."

Amy needed it too, if for no other reason than to understand she serves a loving and forgiving God. When she looks back on those rocky times in her life today, she is thankful for a God who had a plan for her life.

"Why else would I be here today?" she asks. "I'm one of the worst sinners that ever walked on this earth. There's no reason for me to be here except that He has work for me to do. I'll do whatever He asks and go wherever He leads. I owe everything to Him and am nothing without Him. He died for my sins, my terrible sins. How can I not give everything I have to Him?"

Her life changed so much for the better after the MasterLife experience. She was a different person, devoted to the scripture and always listening for a Word from God. Once Chris and Amy turned it over to Him, amazing things began happening. And running – the one constant in Amy's turbulent life – became part of what God would use, as He had intended all along. She became a faith-based runner who would pray and talk with God as she ran. She developed a relationship with Him during those times. The lifestyle that was once filled with nastiness, drugs and alcohol was now full of goodness. Their children are witnessing that great transformation too, and it is impacting them in a good way as well.

Amy's family took 1,200 Christian tracts with them to pass out to whoever would take them in Boston - more than 500,000 are in the city during the marathon weekend. They saw it as a wide-open mission field. Their children passed out tracts and sometimes they'd have them ripped up in front of their faces or thrown down on the ground. But that didn't stop them from passing out more. They had

CHAPTER FOUR

a much more receptive audience the day after the bombs stunned the United States with another terrorist attack.

What Amy did not realize at the time was that the experience at the Boston Marathon was a way for God to open the door for the Amy For Africa mission that in six months raised $43,000 for two schools in impoverished Moyo, Uganda, where Pastor Floyd – the same man who had shepherded them through the MasterLife program – was now on the mission field.

"One of the greatest joys in life, as a teacher, is when you look in someone's eyes and suddenly see the light bulb go off," Paris said. "In that whole group, there was that hunger of 'I want to do what God wants me to do.' Looking back over your past and seeing how God has moved in your life, how God has brought you to this moment, is understanding God's amazing grace."

The more Amy began to reflect on that, the more determined she became to be a disciple of Jesus Christ.

"Anybody that knows Amy knows that once she commits herself to something she does it one hundred percent. Chris's growth was amazing as well. He started out, 'I don't know about this Bible study kind of thing.' It's a commitment to do this. You have assignments you need to do each day, five days a week. She just grew in understanding. In the movie 'Alvin York,' he says 'You don't have the church-going kind of religion; you have the believing kind of religion.' That's what it became for Amy and Chris. She'll always be a runner at heart but she'll be running for God's glory long after the marathon season is over."

MasterLife group from Unity Baptist Church: Bro. Floyd Paris (seated). Back row left: Chris Compston, Amy Compston, Amanda Wesolowski, and Samantha Caudill.

CHAPTER FIVE

LAYING THE GROUNDWORK

God never leads you where He hasn't already laid the groundwork. We learned that lesson during the early days of Amy For Africa.

What we didn't know at the time but figured out later was that God was already putting the pieces in place to make this mission a success. He started working on Amy during the Dayton Air Force Marathon in September 2012. It was her second marathon and she felt His presence during that emotional run. There are photographs of her at mile 18 of the marathon where she is smiling and waving at the camera.

"Anybody that's run even one mile knows if you've run eighteen miles you shouldn't feel like smiling and waving at the camera," she said. "But, man, during that race I really felt His power and His presence. It was amazing. I'd never experienced anything like it. It was God and all Him. I don't know how else to explain it. His power was all over me that day."

Amy knew then and there that God wanted to do something

CHAPTER FIVE

with her running ability. "I didn't know what but I said, 'God, I know you want to use this. I'll do anything you ask me to do.'"

Here's something else we learned: God will use what you love to do for Him. He knows our talents, our skills, and our gifts. He gave them to us to use for Him but only if we are willing.

Amy made it clear that she wanted to use her gift of running for God's glory even if it meant selling bracelets for some of the Christian running groups like Team 413 or Run for God. But she had no idea what was in store for her life-changing summer and how her running ability could be used to raise $43,000 for missions.

It was during the Dayton marathon that Amy ran her fastest marathon and qualified a second time for the Boston Marathon. But qualifying to run doesn't automatically put you in the world's most famous distance race. You have to have a qualifying time but also must be accepted. Amy applied for the Boston Marathon and waited for a reply.

Her first marathon was in Myrtle Beach in February 2012 and she ran a fast enough time to qualify for Boston there as well. That's highly unusual for any distance runner to have a Boston Marathon qualifying time in the first two marathons you participate.

"I'd always been a runner but I hadn't even run a 10K," she said. "The longest run was eight miles and that was in high school. My sister (Traci) did a mini-triathlon and I thought 'If she can do that, I can do a marathon.' I was always afraid of a marathon, intimidated really. I had a friend who did it, John Davis, so I chose to sign up for one. I thought, 'If he can do it, maybe I can do it.' He really encouraged me. My first marathon I qualified for the Boston Marathon and that's so unheard of. I knew we had something here. I knew I was good at this."

LAYING THE GROUNDWORK

She also found out in that marathon how difficult that 26.2 mile journey can be. She didn't properly prepare, including not eating or drinking like she should during the race. At mile 21, she was a wreck. "The worst pain I've ever felt in my life," she said. "At mile 13 I saw my family and was smiling. At mile 16 I was smiling and at mile 21 I was like 'I hate this! I hate this!'"

Her second marathon, in September of 2012, was a much better experience and she credits God for much of the difference.

"I'd surrendered my life to the Lord and let Him train me and teach me how to run. I prepared better, I ate and didn't hit that wall. I could feel God's power in that race. I qualified again (for Boston) and this time it was even better (time). I qualified and got in. My third marathon was going to be the most prestigious marathon in the world."

It was during the time between the Dayton marathon and being accepted for the Boston Marathon that Amy continued to feel certain that God was going to do something big with her running. Her nearly daily hours on the road running also became the place where she grew closer to God. Her faith-based running became part of Amy's trademark and routine. She would read her Bible and then go running. Those runs, sometimes 30 minutes and sometimes five hours, were spent mostly in prayer and fellowship with God. She was drawing near to Him every step of the way.

It wasn't long until she received a notice of acceptance for the Boston Marathon. She had qualified and been invited to run. It was one of the best "natural" highs that Amy had ever experienced. The Boston Marathon is like the Super Bowl of marathons. Every distance runner in the world wants to be part of it. She also knew that many of her running heroes would be participating. She praised God

CHAPTER FIVE

for this "miracle in my life."

But the testing had just begun. Amy and her sister Amanda, their children, and Samantha Caudill and her children went on a fall vacation to Atlantic Beach and during that trip Amy could hardly raise her head off the pillow. She had become terribly ill and the fatigue that had taken over her body was devastating. She was not only unable to run but mostly unable to get out of bed.

When she returned home she saw the doctor and tests revealed she had mononucleosis. It was not welcome news for a runner.

"And how do we react when we get that kind of news? We have a pity party for ourselves and that's what I did. I couldn't believe it," she said. "I was like 'Mono? Really God? Mono?' It can last six weeks, to six months to a year. How was I going to prepare for the Boston Marathon with mono? I was giving up. I went to Pastor Floyd and told him about it. He just looked at me and said 'Amy, what is mono to God?' I said 'You know, you're right.' I went out the next day and tried to run – it was more of a speed walk than a run – but that day I gave it to God. I told Him I was sorry for feeling sorry for myself, that He had allowed me in the Boston Marathon and, even if it's the slowest marathon in the history of the world, I'm there. I praised Him and just gave it to Him."

Amy learned another lesson that day. Once she gave the mono to God, which is all He really wants us to do in the first place, the healing began. By the time she was ready to train for the Boston Marathon, there were no signs of the mono that had ravaged her weeks earlier.

"I was 100 percent completely healed," she said. "From the time I gave it to Him, he started healing me day by day by day until it was all gone. I had some of the best training and best times I'd

LAYING THE GROUNDWORK

ever had."

Still, there was not a word from God on how He was going to use Amy's running. She kept asking and praying about what she was supposed to do, how He wanted to use her gift. The lesson He was teaching her was this: Sometimes the answer is to be patient. God had more groundwork to put down.

It was in December, while practicing for the Living Christmas Tree at Unity Baptist Church, that I overheard Amy's husband talking about her training and acceptance in the Boston Marathon. Even though Chris and Amy had been members of our church since March, I hadn't gotten to know either of them that well. However, as the editor of a daily newspaper in Ashland, Kentucky, I'm always on the lookout for a good story. I asked Chris about the possibility of doing a story on his wife running in the Boston Marathon. He told me she was a bit on the "shy side" but might be open to doing it. I asked Amy in the church kitchen that same night if she would agree to a story and she quickly said yes.

The door was opening for both of us and we never even knew it.

Amy came to my office the following week with her son, Jarek, in tow and I interviewed this bright young woman who was passionate about running and passionate about her faith. She was relaxed, friendly and genuine. It was during that interview that I wondered if Amy could take it a step farther and write a daily diary for the newspaper leading up to the running of the Boston Marathon. My thought was it would be a unique feature for the newspaper.

We ran the story on Amy qualifying for the Boston Marathon – not many in the small area of northeastern Kentucky had ever participated – and readers found it intriguing. The more they talked, the

CHAPTER FIVE

more the idea of the diary stayed with me.

    We have a way of monitoring how many times stories are read online in our digital platform and the hits that original story registered kept my mind open. I asked her about doing the diary for us and she agreed. Amy would chronicle her daily running routine eight weeks leading up to the Boston Marathon in the newspaper. We published a week's worth of the journal every Monday. Each Sunday, Amy handed me several sheets of notebook paper where she had handwritten her thoughts each day after the run. I remember getting it for the first time and thinking 'I wonder if this was a good idea?' I was expecting her to email me the diary but having it handwritten almost spoke to me more. It would be three, four and sometimes five pages of notes, front and back. Luckily, her penmanship was good, most of the time. It was kind of like getting a note passed to you in junior high. She'd walk by me in choir and kind of slip the notes to me. I took the folded package home and unwrapped the thoughts of this faith-based runner in front of my computer. From the very first one, I knew we had something special. There was no way I was going to change the way it was delivered.

    It became a highly popular part of the Monday newspaper because, not only did Amy write about running, but she wrote about her faith. She talked about how she prayed during about 80 percent of her runs and wrote about how her faith had grown so much in the past few months. In a community where there is a church on every corner, it was well received and much appreciated.

    The diary, as it turns out, was almost a test for Amy to prove she was a true follower. It was going to be there for everyone to read, including some of those she worked with at KDMC who she had also had a beer with in the past.

LAYING THE GROUNDWORK

"No one at work knew I was a Christian. This was just February of 2013. No one knew about my faith, my dedication to the Lord. I was still intimidated. When Mark asked me to do this diary, God led me to write about running but also my faith in Him. People were like 'Whoa, I didn't know this side of Amy.' That's when I learned I had to be bold. I am a Christian. Through that story people were really praying for us."

But what neither Amy nor I knew was that it was opening the door to Amy For Africa even a little wider. He wasn't ready for us to step through it, not yet anyway, but He was preparing the way. God is cool that way. Neither of us had any idea that having a story in the newspaper or having a weekly diary would be the gateway to introducing Amy to the Ashland community. They immediately fell in love with her and her commitment to God.

What they didn't know and what I didn't know was her dark past that would soon enough be revealed in her riveting testimony to thousands during the summer.

For now, what everybody knew was that she was a committed runner and a committed Christian. They would learn later about how His healing power completely turned this young woman's life around.

The day before she and her family left for Boston, she took down my cell phone number and promised to call the day of the race. I was figuring one more story on how she finished would be a nice way to close this series of stories. Little did any of us know what would happen during the Boston Marathon.

During the Boston Marathon you can follow the progress of runners electronically online and many of our church family and Amy's friends were doing just that. But when the news broke that

CHAPTER FIVE

two bombs had exploded near the finish line, there were many who had their hearts in their throats. The telephones at the newspaper began ringing off the hook. Everybody, it seemed, had fallen in love with Amy through the stories in the newspaper. They wanted to know:

"Is that girl OK?"

"Is Amy OK?"

"Do you know if Amy was harmed?"

"I sure pray that Amy is OK? Do you know what happened?"

I didn't know if she was OK although it appeared she finished ahead of the bombs. But with everything happening at the finish line, there was no way to know for sure. All cell phone service was cut off and the first word of what happened to Amy came through Facebook. She was unharmed after finishing thirty minutes before the bombs detonated.

She eventually was able to call my cell phone and I spoke with Amy and several family members about what had transpired. We had eyewitnesses to a national tragedy, a terrorist attack on U.S. soil. This young runner who we introduced to the community through a story and diary entrees would be the subject of two more Page 1 stories the day after the Boston Marathon. It was a win for the newspaper is how I figured it.

Her family members, who stood twenty feet from the first bomb for most of the day, also escaped harm. Twenty-one of them, including eleven children stood near a Starbucks and used the coffee place's restroom facilities many times throughout the day, as you might expect with eleven children. That Starbucks had its windows blown out and inside destroyed from the bomb's force.

None of Amy's family saw any of the carnage although they

LAYING THE GROUNDWORK

did hear the noise. "I praise God today that He spared them from seeing any of that," she said. "He kept them safe and led them down the alley. If they had gone left or right, they would have been hit. But He led them down that alley."

Amy and Chris were away from the bombs. Runners are ushered to a waiting area to meet with a family member after finishing the race. They didn't know what had happened although the panic in the crowd had already set in. Then they found out but also quickly learned that their family had escaped harm. It was a time of chaos in Boston but the family finally was all together again after a subway ride back to where they were staying. The emotions of the day overwhelmed Amy who could do nothing but cry. The most triumphant day of her life also became one of sadness and thankfulness. For some reason, God had spared her and her family. Was it fate? Was it luck? Or was it God's will because of what He had in store? Remember, at this point, Amy For Africa hadn't even started.

"He spared me because He has work for me to do," she said.

God was building the foundation for the mission. Some asked where was God in the midst of the tragedy and chaos during the Boston Marathon? But Amy and her family felt the Almighty's presence. They felt it on the streets of Boston before the race while passing out Christian tracts to anybody who would take them.

The day after the race, when returning to the city, they didn't feel the same fear that many others did. They kept passing out tracts and this time their audience had become more attentive and receptive. Her children would take them up to officers and soldiers who were carrying loaded machine guns.

"We knew God was watching over us," Amy said. "We weren't worried about something happening."

CHAPTER FIVE

Maybe they were naïve or maybe God provided them with that peace that passes all understanding.

Amy knew this much: He had work for her to do. But what was it going to be?

They returned home the following day and she was met with a hero's welcome. Her yard was decorated with cards from her work friends. Her church was decorated with cards from her church family. The community was happy that they all made it back unharmed after being in the midst of this national tragedy.

If they had missed the stories before, they surely knew it now. Amy was gaining some "celebrity status" in the area because of what had happened.

About two weeks before the Boston Marathon, during a training run, she had a "conversation with God" about running for missions. She made a "deal with God" that if she didn't have any injuries in Boston, she would run a 50-mile race for missions.

"I don't know why we try to make deals with God because He's always going to get His way," she said later. "But that's what I did. Well, not only did I not get hurt in Boston but I ran my best time ever and escaped two bombs and a literal terrorist attack! I was like, 'OK God, I get it! I'll run for missions.'"

Two days after returning home she signed up for the Nashville Ultra-Marathon 50-mile race. She wasn't doing it for any personal glory but for missions and specifically missions in Moyo, Uganda.

She had seen the need in Moyo through photographs and videos that Brother Floyd had put together. Amy's heart broke when she saw the "babies," as she calls them, from Moyo without much clothing and hardly any food. Amy fell in love with those "sweet babies" and even then determined in her mind that she was going to

LAYING THE GROUNDWORK

help. She and Chris even considered adopting a child but the Ugandan red tape kept that from getting very far. Even though Amy didn't know it, that's when the seed was sown for where the funds would go from donations to Amy For Africa. United Christian Expeditions that sponsors two Penne Paris schools in Moyo seemed the perfect fit for any fundraising efforts. She learned about UCE, which was started by Floyd Paris as a non-profit in early 2012, during MasterLife class. That's where Amy's heart was to raise the money.

"I asked the MasterLife group to pray with me because we needed to find somebody who can be there," Paris said. "I have a Ph.D. in missions and have been there since day one. Who better to go than me? But there's no way I can do that. I'm too old to be a Southern Baptist missionary and there's no organization raising money in support of me."

That's when God tugged on Amy's heart. "She said, 'I'd like to raise money for that.' She got involved then with Mark Maynard, our chairman of the deacons. God kind of put them together. He has a lot of connections, knows a lot of people as the editor of our local paper. The Lord just began to open doors. They began to raise a substantial amount of money. I thought, 'Praise the Lord!' As I was talking to my children about Dad going over to Africa, my son, Philip, said 'Dad, you can't go unless somebody is here raising money for you.' I told him, 'Amy For Africa is raising quite a bit of money and the Lord just might be in this. I can raise money when I'm home and she can raise it when I'm not here.'"

Amy wasn't sure how this mission fundraising effort was going to work. Could she get friends and family to donate per mile on the 50-mile race? Or was there a better way?

She came to me with her questions and asked if I would help

CHAPTER FIVE

her set up a platform. I'm not even sure why to this day I said yes, except that God was tugging at my heart to help too. I saw it as a challenge, too, as a way to use what I am gifted at doing for Him. Maybe that was it as much as anything. God will use what you love doing if you will allow it to happen. He gives each of his talents and gifts and the ultimate plan is to use those for His glory. Sometimes we do and sometimes we don't. But this time, for whatever reason, I saw it as an opportunity to use my gift that He so blessed me with all these years.

The groundwork had been laid long before either Amy or I ever knew it or even knew each other. But God knew it. He prepares the way for you even when you don't realize it. Looking back on it now, it's easy to see how it happened. With each building block, He also taught us lessons on being patient, on being faithful and never underestimating His power in all things.

Amy crosses the finish line in the Air
Force Marathon in Dayton, Ohio,
in September 2012.

One of Amy's early speaking assignments to the
Ashland High School classes from the 1940s.
She wowed them with her testimony.

CHAPTER SIX

TURNING IT OVER TO GOD

So much happened during the summer of 2013 that let us know Amy For Africa was going to be blessed by God. We saw Him at work almost every day of the journey and received so much spiritual strength from what we were witnessing.

It started almost immediately, too, after deciding a goal of trying to raise $10,000 for the United Christian Expeditions.

With what happened at Boston and Amy being in the midst of it, finding a hook for her platform was rather easy. Lots of people would want to hear this story, but we needed more to have a fundraiser of any financial substance.

In today's world, you need the hook but you also need an online presence. I told Amy that we needed to build a website and I had somebody in mind to do it, but it wasn't going to be free.

She agreed we needed the website and asked Brother Floyd about the possibility. He told her that our church's webmaster, youth director Brad Callaway, could put something together and it wouldn't cost anything. Amy got back with me and said maybe that would be

CHAPTER SIX

the best option. For one of the few times in our partnership, I really did not agree with her. I wanted Adam VanKirk, our lead designer at the newspaper, who also runs a graphic business on the side, to become involved. Brad had more than enough on his plate at church and, for this to work well, this website was going to need multiple functions and would be the centerpiece for fundraising. Adam wasn't going to charge much so I told Amy I'd pay for half the install and we'd ask for donations to raise the rest. The startup was only going to be about $300 and Adam's creativeness was worth far more than that.

Eventually, Amy saw it my way and we met with Adam one afternoon and started the plans in motions. It was Adam who came up with the "Amy For Africa" name for the website. We tossed around several ideas but that one seemed to fit. Amy didn't like it because she didn't want the platform to be "all about me." We assured her that wouldn't be the case but "Amy For Africa" had a certain ring to it that would work. She reluctantly agreed to let her name be used, and the website planning began.

I asked Amy about a fundraising goal and foolishly said to her. "Well, what do you think? Maybe $1,000 or $2,000 as a goal?"

She quickly replied, "Mark? $5,000, $10,000! We shouldn't underestimate what God can do."

I thought to myself that Amy was thinking too big but I said, "OK, let's go $10,000!" But, honestly, that kind of goal seemed impossible and improbable. But I didn't want to temper her enthusiasm.

Our first talk to a civic group was the East Greenup County Kiwanis Club at the Giovanni's in Flatwoods. Amy shared her story of Boston and then a riveting testimony of her life with alcohol and

TURNING IT OVER TO GOD

drugs that I'd never heard. I'm sure my jaw was on the table as she told layer by layer of how her life for fourteen years had become a mess. It was then and there that I thought to myself, "Oh my, we have something here. More people need to hear this testimony. This word has to get out."

With the connections that I've established in the Ashland area through my job at the newspaper since 1975, and my position in the working and religious communities in the Ashland area, I have some connections. Amy's "speaking tour" filled easily and quickly.

We added a layer to the speaking with a brief slideshow video that was essentially Amy's life from a young girl until now, including those rough times when she was abusing alcohol and drugs. There were photos of she and Amanda living the party life that were graphic and almost shocking. Matthew West's "Story of My Life" played in the background of the video.

The photos from the reckless lifestyle came from Amanda, who found them in the back of a closest in a box marked "The Past." She pulled them out and looked at them almost with disgust. The next question: Would she allow her sister to use them in the video that many were going to be watching?

"The first video Amy put on for Amy For Africa have many pictures of me doing drugs with pipes and alcohol," Amanda said. "When she asked me can I use these of me I had to think about it. Do I want my pictures for everyone to see? It was amazing I still had them. I thought 'Why do I still have these?' I figured they must need to be used. Why else take a picture of yourself doing drugs? She said 'You're sure I can tell Mark to put these pictures in the video?' I told her to do it. Number one, it will keep me from ever doing it again. It will keep me accountable. Go ahead and use them."

CHAPTER SIX

Amanda said the video can be hard for her to watch. The happiness in the photographs is short-lived, she said. "It looks like we're having a blast but I look at those now and think what emptiness, what were we trying to find in drugs and alcohol? It was fun at the time but it was short term. You don't have to find love or desire in drugs or alcohol. It takes you down a road you don't want to be on."

The video was a powerful ending to Amy's testimony. She explained that we will all have our life story played at the throne of Jesus Christ. What will your life story look like?

Amy's delivery and comfortableness at speaking in front of crowds improved with each appearance. God was working and we both knew it. Audiences were intently listening and hanging on her every word. Her testimony of how she started running as a young girl and then how drug and alcohol addiction nearly ruined her life seemed to resonate. Everybody knew somebody, or had a family member, dealing with similar drug experiences. It has become so commonplace in eastern Kentucky and really throughout the country. Lives are being ruined on a daily basis. Amy and her family are lucky that they are not part of those statistics today. Her testimony of God's grace in her life was giving hope to the hopeless.

Amy visits with Rep. Tanya Pullin in
Frankfort in August 2013.

Amy with her son, Bear, during
a radio interview on WLGC.

Amy and her family in front of the state capitol in August 2013.

CHAPTER SEVEN
THE MISSION

From the very beginning of what is turning out to be a lifelong journey, Amy was always ready and willing to speak with anybody about her life and this mission. We went before her bosses – the executives at King's Daughters Medical Center – where she spoke openly about overcoming her problems with drugs and alcohol. And, remember, through ten years of her addiction she was employed by KDMC.

But Amy's turnaround and ability to tell her story in such a genuine way made her an amazing speaker. Even though there were times when she was admittedly nervous, like standing in front of the KDMC executives, it never showed. She kept her composure and emotions in check and simply shared her testimony.

Our first time in front of a church congregation came at First Baptist Church in downtown Ashland. We met before she spoke with pastor Harold Moore in his office. We certainly felt God's presence in that place. She had spoken to several civic groups by that time and was comfortable with what she was going to say.

No matter where we went, Amy packed a giant file folder with her. I think it had a little bit of everything in it, including some notes

CHAPTER SEVEN

she'd scribbled out but hardly ever had to use. She took those up to the podium with her, along with her Bible, and let it fly.

Her mother, stepfather Bob Whitely, Chris, Amanda and her daughter Reagan and Amy's children – Skylar, Bailee, Bear and Jarek – all went with us that week. We pretty much packed a pew.

Our routine at the churches where we spoke was for me to briefly introduce Amy and our mission and then she spoke for about twenty to thirty minutes. She made it clear and often said that she wasn't preacher but a witness to what Jesus Christ had done in her life. Nobody was ever offended, that we knew of, about her speaking in front of the church. That's good, too, because there's no question that God is using this young woman in a powerful way through her words.

The visit to First Baptist Church in Ashland was such a blessing and turned out to be the start of a generous fundraising week, something which we never expected to happen.

Part of the congregation at First Baptist included some visitors from Hopewell Baptist Church, which is located in the Charlotte, North Carolina, area. They were in Ashland as part of a mission project team. They had chosen Ashland as a mission area and God allowed us to be part of that with them.

A few weeks before they came to Ashland, the leader of their group, Larry Furr, came to the newspaper offices looking for some information on purchasing an advertisement about a concert the group would be putting on at the end of their mission effort.

For whatever reason – and I'm pretty sure it was a divine appointment – Larry ended up in my office. I have nothing to do with advertisements at the newspaper. But God directed Larry to my office anyway. We met and talked, found out we had much in common

THE MISSION

and began a friendship that remains strong today. He told me about his mission trip to Ashland and I told him about Amy For Africa.

Larry immediately bought into what we were doing and asked if Amy would speak at the concert. I told them she'd be glad to do it. I didn't have to run it past Amy, that's just how we rolled in Amy For Africa. Amy never questioned any move I made when it came to this project. Not even once. I told her where we were going and she said I'll be ready.

We had a partnership with our relationship and became close friends throughout the journey. Our spouses could only shake their heads at the number of texts we would send to each other. Less understanding spouses would probably have been suspicious that something more was going on between us. But the only thing happening was a partnership with Amy For Africa that was becoming bigger than either one of us expected it to be.

When Larry Furr was in my office, I also told him about our church's Judgment House program that would be going on the week his mission team was in town. We made his team some reservations and many of those who came to the church service at First Baptist Church that morning had been to Unity the previous night.

They had no idea that Amy was going to be speaking at First Baptist but it was so nice to see them that morning in their bright green shirts. It was like we had even more friends in the house. There were many good folks at the church that I already knew, including Charlie Chatfield. who helped set up our visit to First Baptist. He and his wife, Janet, are such sweet, generous people. They made an impact with Amy For Africa in many ways and we appreciate them so much.

That day at First Baptist Church they took up a love offering

CHAPTER SEVEN

for Amy For Africa. We found out the following day that it was more than $800 and were overwhelmed. The day after that, I received an early morning text from Larry Furr who said his church's mission committee had decided to give $1,000 to Amy For Africa. The day following that I received a call from Jay Hutchinson, a member at First Baptist, who told me the church was giving us another sizeable donation. It was from that week that we realized how much God was in this mission and how foolish setting a goal of $1,000 to $2,000 really was.

Everything seemed to start rolling from that point, including traveling practically every Sunday morning and night to a church in the area. Everyone was so welcoming and so giving that our hearts were warmed and encouraged each and every week. But we didn't stop at the church community for fundraising help. We planned events, including a three-on-three whiffle ball tournament in the side lot of the church that raised nearly $2,000. Big Sandy Superstores co-sponsored the whiffle ball tournament and Chick-fil-A had become a sponsor for Amy For Africa as well, including giving us proceeds from chicken biscuits and sandwiches they sold at the whiffle ball tournament. WLGC's Cross Section radio show also adopted Amy. She spoke several times, giving us yet another platform. During a talk to the Ashland Rotary Club, city commissioners Cheryl Spriggs and Marty Gute presented Amy with a Key to the City of Ashland. Everybody in the Ashland area was learning about Amy and the Amy For Africa mission.

Within a couple of weeks of launching the website we were approaching $5,000 and within eight weeks it was past the original goal of $10,000. We knew this much for sure: God's hand was in this work.

THE MISSION

Local businessman Bob Hammond challenged Amy's son Bear to a 5K race in downtown Ashland during a planned First Friday run. Together they raised more than $1,200 for the cause with a voting contest. You could vote for either Bob or Bear to win online for $1. It generated some buzz throughout the community. By the way, Bear not only crushed Bob in fundraising but held him off in the 5K.

In the middle of August, Amy and her family, along with me and Beth, made a trip to Frankfort to be recognized on the floor of the House of Representatives by Majority Floor Leader Rocky Adkins and Representative Kevin Sinnette. It was an amazing honor for Amy, who stood proud as they read a proclamation about what she had already accomplished and how she'd overcome drugs and alcohol.

The House floor was a little noisy, as is typical, during the reading until it got to the part about the drugs and alcohol. That's when the representatives in the room turned and listened. By the time Adkins and Sinnette had finished reading the proclamation, the lawmakers broke into a standing ovation for Amy. Several of them came up to shake her hand and have their photograph taken with her.

The following March, state Senator Robin Webb invited Amy to be recognized on the Senate floor for all that she had done with the mission. Amy was accompanied by me, her mother, father and his wife Teresa. It was another day of celebration for Amy For Africa.

The mission was infiltrating beyond the small community of Ashland, Kentucky. It had now reached some celebrity status in the state capitol.

One of the most emotional moments of the summer came when we shared Amy For Africa with our own church, Unity Baptist.

CHAPTER SEVEN

We had already done several others and it was probably a good thing because that better prepared us for our own folks.

It was also emotional because, by that time, Brother Floyd had announced his decision to leave as pastor of Unity Baptist Church and become a fulltime missionary in Moyo, Uganda, which is where the Amy For Africa funds were going.

Brother Floyd, of course, was at the service. It went as smoothly at Unity as it has gone anywhere although Amy was a little more emotional than usual. But she held her composure and delivered the same speech that had gripped so many other audiences. After the service we put out an "envelope challenge" to our congregation. We laid out one hundred envelopes with Amy For Africa logos on the front and a slip of paper with a dollar amount from $1 to $100 on the inside.

We asked members to take an envelope and donate whatever the slip of paper had written on it. Nobody would have to give more than $100 (although one couple in the church drew out the $100 and the $99). That resulted in a nearly $5,000 donation from our church. At that time, our total had grown to more than $20,000 and our new goal was set at $40,000. It was a good start to the new goal.

Unity was so supportive of the mission even beyond the envelope challenge. Many individuals had already given to the cause and many of them took an envelope anyway. There is no more giving church than Unity Baptist and they saw the impact that the Amy For Africa mission was having on the community and even inside their own church walls. They were proud that the Unity family was a part of Amy For Africa and still are today.

It's fitting considering that for more than twenty years, since former pastor Harold and his wife Beverly Cathey journeyed to

THE MISSION

Uganda to become fulltime missionaries, our church has supported missions in Africa. We also sent out Diana Ferrell as a fulltime missionary to Uganda and she remains on the mission field there today. John Fulks is another fulltime missionary supported by the church.

Amy For Africa seemed like a natural extension of what had already been put in place.

We were able to get into several schools including presenting the message five times to classes at Fairview junior high and high school. She also spoke to FCA groups in Ashland schools and we traveled about an hour for a class at Blaine Elementary in Lawrence County. It was on the way home from that trip that Amy received a text from Janie Smith, the secretary at Unity. She had received a check for the mission and wanted to tell Amy over the phone and not by text what had come in the mail. We were sitting at around $33,000 at that time with about four days left before leaving for the Ultra-Marathon in Nashville. Janie told Amy that the check from the Lowman Foundation was for $5,000! It was such a special moment that we were able to share together in the car on the ride home. At that point, we knew the rest of the total was going to come – and it did.

Amy and son Jarek at a 5K in downtown Ashland in August 2013. Jarek's hair was painted Amy For Africa green.

Ryan Lynch kisses the trophy after L-Train captured the inaugural Amy For Africa Whiffle Ball Tournament in August 2013. Adam Lalonde, left, and Rob Lynch were part of the winning team.

Amy stands with some of the crew from Orange Leaf which provided one of the many donations from the Ashland community.

Amy For Africa supporters Beth Maynard, left, and Kathy Whitely at a local race in Ashland. Beth is the wife of Mark Maynard and Kathy is Amy's mother.

Amy speaks at an anti-drug rally.

Amy and Mark are interviewed on Ohio Southern
University's Horizon program.

Amy speaks with a FCA group at Ashland Blazer
in September 2013.

Chris runs beside Bear to help pace him to
victory during a 5K run in Ashland in
August 2013. Bear helped raised $1,200 in the race.

CHAPTER EIGHT
THE UNSUNG HEROES

Throughout the first five months of the Amy For Africa mission, one man stood on the outside looking in. It was Amy's husband, Chris, a kind-hearted individual who was happy when his wife was happy. Nobody was prouder of Amy than Chris. He positively glowed at the mere mention of her name or when she came in the room. True love had him. Chris gave up a lot of his own time during the mission effort, being left for diaper duty for young Jarek or even having to put his wants and wishes on the back-burner. Amy had the outlet of running. It was a time when she got away from everything and everyone, including Chris. The streets of Ashland were her sanctuary for runs that would take three, four and even five hours.

Meanwhile, somebody was home with the four children and that somebody was often Chris. We jokingly introduced him as "Amy's husband" instead of Chris on the many times when he went to speak with us. Chris smiled and waved to the congregations. Truth be told, though, Chris was enjoying this Amy For Africa mission and its amazing growth as much as anybody. He told Amy early on in the project, when the fundraising total was around $5,000, not to be too disappointed if the mission doesn't generate any more than that.

CHAPTER EIGHT

The original goal was $10,000 and Chris could be counted among the doubters. But as the money kept coming in, he saw the kind of power that was harnessed by God. He became a confirmed believer in Amy For Africa and also learned the lesson of who was in control of every situation. It became a God moment for him.

As the months rolled on and as Amy's celebrity status grew, at least in and around the Ashland area, her time away from home became more and more necessary. It wasn't always Chris who watched the kids though. After all, he also worked a fulltime nurse's job at King's Daughters Medical Center. Skylar, the oldest of the four children, did more than most 13-year-olds should be expected to do. She would mother Jarek and bark orders at Bailee and Bear. They knew to mind her, too. Skylar is mature beyond her years, a precious young woman with a heart of gold and a love of God that will serve her for years to come. Her presence in the home is another reason that Amy was able to run whenever she needed and for as long as she needed. Chris's mother, Tammy Howard, and Amy's mother, Kathy Whitely, were other necessary babysitters when needed, especially for Jarek. Chris's mother lives in Ashland so there were many mornings when she would keep Jarek so Amy could get some sleep after working a midnight shift at the hospital. Rest is as essential to a runner as it is to you and me. Without these family members, and others, like her sister Amanda Evans, the Amy For Africa mission and Amy's training for a 50-mile ultra marathon would have been difficult, if not impossible.

A mission like this has no power without pray warriors and we have two of the best in my wife Beth and Amy's mother Kathy. Every step of the journey has been literally bathed in prayer by these two faithful servants of God. Amy's father is another diligent supporter even though he lives nearly two hours from Ashland. Steve believes in his daughter and he believes in the Christian tract ministry. His church, Landmark Baptist in Winchester, Kentucky, purchased 10,000 tracts for the Amy For Africa mission's 2014 venture.

Amy asked her family after the Boston Marathon if they were onboard with her training for an ultra marathon. She knew the kind of commitment it was going to take. Everybody agreed it was what she needed to do next and everybody understood there would be sacrifices made, even the young ones.

Amy is always quick to recognize her many helpers during the time when she was either running, speaking, working, praying or sleeping. Those five things became her priority, along with daily Bible readings and a steaming cup of coffee. Other things would have to wait and it wasn't always easy on the family life. She gave them the time she could but there are only so many hours in the day. The children learned to be independent to a degree although, if discipline was needed, Amy and Chris were both quick to dispatch it. What these children are now learning from their parents is the importance of serving the King of Kings and putting other's need above their own. It's a lesson that many parents need to teach their own children in this day of entitlement.

God wants our addictions, our problems, our troubles, our gifts, our praise ... everything about us. He wants it all and then he wants us to get out of the way. That's what Amy Compston did. She let the Holy Spirit work inside her and she began to blossom into a sold-out, bold witness for the Lord Jesus Christ. Her story isn't a pretty one but it's a real one. But it was the kind of transformation that those on the outside, those of the world, can see, too. What has happened to her? That's what they're saying today. What happened

CHAPTER EIGHT

was she gave it all to God — all the bad and all the good. And she's hardly a finished product. God has a new soldier in His Army and she can run like the wind.

Amy Compston runs with her children and nieces and nephews during the Nashville Ultra-Marathon in November 2013. This was at mile 36 of the 50-mile race.

Amy's sister, Amanda Wesolowski, was an important cog in the Amy For Africa team even though whiffle ball wasn't her strong suit.

Amy Compston and Mark Maynard started the Amy For Africa mission in May 2013.

Amy and Chris at the rainy Ashland Christmas Parade in November 2013.

CHAPTER NINE

A MOMENT TO REMEMBER

For about two weeks prior to the Nashville Ultra Marathon, Chris began doing a little running of his own around Ashland. He would go on runs of five or six miles, at the most, just enough to keep in some kind of running shape.

Because ultra marathons allow friends or family to jump in and run with the competitors, Chris wanted to experience some of the thrill if Amy needed some company. If she didn't want any company, that was fine with him, too. But he wanted to be ready just in case.

Two days before the ultra marathon was "carb-load day" for Amy and Chris decided to join her. Carb-load day is probably the best day to be a runner because you mostly eat everything in sight. Chris and Amy plowed through a couple of bags of Twizzlers and Starbursts – both loaded with sugar and carbohydrates – on the way to Williamsburg where Amy was speaking later at the University of Cumberlands. That's where Julie Paris, daughter of Floyd Paris, goes to college. Julie, of course, is one of the founders of the Penne Paris

CHAPTER NINE

Schools in Moyo, Uganda. So the Amy For Africa team's appearance at the college seemed to bring the mission full circle, since the Penne Paris Schools was the recipient of the fundraising.

The morning after speaking, Chris and Amy even went on a two-mile jog together around Williamsburg. Little did they know what would transpire one day later in Nashville.

Chris woke up early on Race Day and began preparing himself just in case. He was dressed and ready to run at any juncture of the race. He promised himself that 1) He would only run if Amy asked him and 2) He would not cross the finish line with her. Chris wanted no attention on him. This was Amy's day and it was Amy's race. It turned out to be a day this Christian couple will likely never forget.

Not only was Chris determined to be ready to jump into the race at any time, he was also determined not to miss seeing Amy run past him at the many checkpoints along the race route. The day before the race, when a group of us went with Amy to pick up her racing bib, we picked up street directions on how to get to these checkpoints. Since none of us knew the Nashville area well, we needed some kind of direction. Chris would jump in his van – "The Silver Bullet" – and race around to the many stops. He was itching to run and you could tell it. But he wasn't going to unless Amy asked. He knew his wife and he knew she'd ask if it was necessary.

Chris was like somebody whose feet were on fire. He was pacing at every stop and relieved every time he saw Amy's smiling face come around the corner. He was so zoned in on the race I'm surprised all four of the children who were in tow with him all made it to the destinations. For that, Chris and Amy can thank grandmothers, aunts and uncles, nieces, friends, and the siblings themselves. When Amy For Africa travels, they come in waves.

A MOMENT TO REMEMBER

It was at the turn around mile thirty-six that Chris got the call from Amy to join her. She had never run more than thirty-one miles in her life and the fatigue was beginning to set in. Chris was out of his sweats in about two seconds and running off with Amy. In his mind, the plan was to run about five to eight miles and then meet some of us at one of the two remaining checkpoints.

Everybody piled in our respective vehicles and headed off to the next stop, a walking bridge near LP Stadium, where the Tennessee Titans play, in the downtown Nashville area. The runners came over the bridge about five or six miles past the last checkpoint. Isolated dark clouds were forming almost, it seemed, right over the area where the runners would be crossing the bridge. The skies opened up and everybody ran for cover. Beth and Julie were midway up the bridge, where they were going to signal us when Amy and Chris approached. They were caught in the middle of the storm but Beth protected them with a blanket she had taken along. They made a fort out of it and kneeled down until the storms passed. Unfortunately, they never saw Chris and Amy pass by them. Because of other events going on in and around Nashville, it wasn't easy getting around. As a matter of fact, only one group, ours, made it to the checkpoint at the bridge.

With the rain pouring down, Chris and Amy came over the bridge together and Amy had the biggest smile on her face. "I asked the Lord for rain at mile 40! This is such a blessing from God!" While everybody else was running for cover, and Beth and Julie were huddled together under a homemade blanket fort, Amy was praising God for the showers of blessing that were pelting her tired body.

As Chris made the turn at the bottom of the bridge, he uttered through shortened breath, "She is amazing! Unreal! Amazing! I love

CHAPTER NINE

her so much!"

There was no way Chris was stopping there. He would wait for the next checkpoint and let Amy finish the last five miles by herself through some wooded area. At least that was his plan. Chris knew he was reaching his limit, that he'd never run more than 10 miles without severe cramping. He ran and finished the Dayton Air Force Marathon but had to stop and walk after 10 miles because the cramps wouldn't allow his body to continue running. Runners call it hitting the wall. That was in the back of his mind as they headed toward the next checkpoint. But he figured he could gut it out for Amy.

The only problem with his plan was that nobody could get to the next checkpoint because of street traffic. We waited 15 minutes to cross the street at LP Stadium because of a 600-motorcycle caravan for Toys for Tots. It was amazing to see but we knew Chris was going to be greeted with no one and that he was going to have to finish the rest of the race. He could have dropped out, of course, at any point but he was determined to go as far as physically possible.

Remember, he had done some running prior to the ultra marathon and it was definitely a good thing. While Chris had been running a little, completing a half marathon with next to no preparation was not going to be easy and he knew it. The cramps started coming and Chris, at times running a few feet behind Amy, remembered how his wife had talked about the tough times and how she dealt with it. He began quoting scripture and singing church hymns. Amy joined with him and cried out to God for strength while running through a wooded area, one of the toughest parts of the course. Amy said her legs were so numb she almost could not lift them over a log in the pathway. They were both struggling but determined to complete this mighty task. "It was amazing the strength that came from quoting those scriptures and singing the hymns," Chris said. "It was just like Amy said."

Amy remembers crying out to God, "Help us Father! Strengthen us Father!" God did deliver them from their pain and kept Amy going. Even better, the couple was able to share God's amazing power together.

They were able to keep running at Amy's nine-minute per mile pace during the entire time Chris was running with her. Not only was he running, but he was going at an accelerated pace. The fatigue and fear of cramps began about two miles from the finish line. Chris could go no further at Amy's pace. He told her to "go on." The rest of the race was all Amy which, in reality, is what Chris wanted.

Amy came through the tunnel on the last stretch of the race to cheering Amy for Africa fans. The children, carrying the Amy for Africa banner behind her, followed her to the finish line. There was such a smile on her face as she finished in a slow sprint. She literally had left everything on the course. She lifted up her arms in triumph as family and friends surrounded her and offered congratulatory hugs. It was an emotional moment for everyone involved. Five months of training had come down to this moment.

A few minutes later, up walked Chris, her exhausted husband. He didn't get the greeting that Amy received although everybody knew Chris Compston was a hero of the day, too. God used him to give Amy a lift just when she needed it and kept her at a pace that allowed her to complete the race in seven hours, thirty-six minutes and fourteen seconds, good enough for second among all female participants and ahead of all but five of the male participants. The happy couple embraced at the finish line and anybody watching who didn't tear up just a little is lying. Chris was Amy's rock when she needed

CHAPTER NINE

it. He did what spouses are supposed to do. They are to be supportive, uplifting and inspiring. Chris was all that and more. He wanted no credit for what transpired but, truly, Chris made a difference in Amy's race. She would have finished the race no matter what but being able to share those 12 miles with him made it all the more special, especially during the times when they both simply cried out to God for his sustaining strength. It's a moment in their lives that will be frozen in time.

Amy at the Nashville Ultra-Marathon in November 2013.

Chris joins Amy for mile 40 (when the rain came) at the Nashville Ultra Marathon.

Amy hugs her sister Traci Vazquez after the Nashville Ultra Marathon in November 2013.

Amy during the Nashville Ultra Marathon with nephews carrying the banner behind her.

Amy Compston nears the finish line in the Nashville Ultra-Marathon with a parade of children behind her.

CHAPTER TEN
BRINGING A FAMILY TOGETHER AGAIN

Amy For Africa did a lot for many people in the summer of 2013 but maybe received more blessing from it than Amy's own family. They became reunited through her efforts, enjoying each other's company again and drawing closer to God because of it.

The family that had been through so much anger, bitterness and resentment was coming together under a common goal – Amy Compston's running. They vacationed together in Boston and again in Nashville, staying in the same homes and being a family again.

Amanda Evans gets choked up at what has transpired for her family.

"Amy For Africa has been amazing," she said. "I never dreamed it could be so big. I never dreamed what God would do with it. He has shown His power and His amazing grace so abundantly. I have seen Amy encourage not only our family but so many others in the community."

Watching her sister bare her soul to anyone who would listen was inspiring, Amanda said. "She was so completely, brutally honest

CHAPTER TEN

that people didn't know what to think. They were in awe of the story itself and encouraged because you can overcome with Christ. She proved that through everything you're able to overcome all these obstacles because of Jesus Christ."

But another benefit was how Amy For Africa reunited a family in a way that Amanda said she thought would never happen.

"When Mom and Dad got divorced there were years of anger, bitterness, resentfulness. Over the years we had gotten our relationships back little by little. When Amy For Africa happened, we all jumped on board, we were supportive, we started loving each other again. Because Christ loves us, we see it, how much He loves this mission, how much He loves Amy, what he's doing for each one of us. As a family, we were whole again. I never dreamed in a million years we would go on family vacation twice in one year - Mom, Dad, their spouses, our entire family - and just have the best time. It reminded me when we were kids. We could talk and laugh. It was great."

Kathy said Amy For Africa has been a blessing to so many but none more than her family.

"Amy For Africa, the whole ministry itself, has really blessed our family. We have family in Chicago, family in Lexington and the family here. It has brought us all together. We decided to go to Boston first and didn't know if the Chicago people were going to come. They couldn't stand it and had to show up there. That made us all in the house together. Then, when we decided to do Amy For Africa, we all had this common goal to see her succeed in her running and see these children fed in Africa. Her brother, he was very skeptical at first, because he didn't know what Amy was doing. I tried to talk to him, 'Andy, you've got to hear her testimony and you

BRINGING A FAMILY TOGETHER AGAIN

will understand everything.' He did get to hear her testimony and it broke his heart."

The family all went to Nashville to support Amy in the 50-mile run, too. It was while staying there that, on the night before the race, Amy shared her testimony to a family audience for those who hadn't heard it. You could have heard a pin drop in the crowded room as Amy eloquently spoke her heart.

"That evening we gathered around and Mark and Amy spoke. Mark introduced Amy like he did every single time they spoke and Amy gave her testimony. It touched our family's heart. They realized then what this was about. They understood why she was doing it. God can do such great things in a life, a willing life, one that's ready to serve."

CHAPTER ELEVEN

RESULTS OF A MISSION (HOW YOU CAN HELP)

The Great Commission tells us to go tell and that's exactly what Amy For Africa did in 2013 in a big way.

Amy Compston juggled a training schedule of 1,266 miles with speaking engagements at many churches, civic groups, recovery groups, detention centers and even the Kentucky House of Representatives. Amy shared not only about Africa but how God rescued this fulltime nurse, wife and mother of four from 14 years of drug and alcohol addiction.

The mission team raised more than $43,000 in six months, culminating with Amy's second-place finish in the Nashville Ultra Marathon.

Every cent of the money raised went directly to Moyo, Uganda, through the United Christian Expeditions, under the direction of Dr. Floyd Paris, and it was immediately put to good use in this remote area.

Money was used to send five hundred ninety seven students through school and feed them a meal every day. It also paid for

CHAPTER ELEVEN

teacher salaries for 2014 for three schools, including the two Penne Paris Schools. The mission also took on expenses for the Moyo Babies Home and its 78 children and supplied the medical needs for the nearly 600 students in the schools and the orphanage.

Chicken coups and fences were built for the orphanage so they can raise their own food. God's love has been sweeping through the area through what has happened with Amy For Africa and, for that we can only say thank you to the many who donated. The impact in that area has been amazing with land being given to UCE by a local to build more schools.

Forty-two medical clinics and one hospital were stocked with supplies and the government also gave UCE permission to go into any hospital. The clinics see anywhere from 150 to 300 patients every day.

Because of the generous donations of the supporters of the Amy For Africa mission, the area of Moyo now has hope. God's love has been shared and these young children are finding out about Jesus Christ.

God has graciously allowed us to know of at least 74 who have come to know Him through the Amy For Africa mission.

That's why we're not stopping now. In 2014, Amy returned to run in the Boston Marathon. That was the first of eight marathons she was scheduled to run in eight months. The Chicago Marathon and New York City Marathon, both world marathons like Boston, were also on the docket.

Amy For Africa has taken on 501(3) (c) non-profit status in 2014 and will continue to fund UCE and other projects in the African nation through the donations.

The goal is to continue speaking at churches with Amy sharing

RESULTS OF A MISSION

her grace story, how God healed her from drug and alcohol abuse, and share the need of the people in Africa.

Amy is asking her friends and anyone else who comes across the website to pray about what God may want them to give in her quest to assist the children in Moyo.

You can be involved by donating to Amy For Africa through the website (amyforafrica.com) or by mailing a check to 816 23rd Street, Ashland, Kentucky 41101. Any donation will be tax deductible.

Amy is running for Africa. Will you run with her?

Some of the children in Moyo, Uganda.

Paster Floyd Paris talks to students at the Penne Paris School, wearing his Amy For Africa shirt.

This is what the Amy For Africa mission is all about.

Piercing eyes from Moyo, Uganda inspire the
Amy For Africa team to do as much as they can.

CHAPTER TWELVE
A FINAL WORD

Amy Compston's grace story is certainly one full of drama, how she learned how to be a disciple for Christ at the age of twenty-eight after being an infant and immature Christian for nearly nineteen years.

Amy can remember the exact place and time when she came to know Jesus Christ, at nine years old, kneeling at her father's bedside. However, she remained an "infant Christian" for much of her life. It wasn't until she realized the power of the Holy Spirit, which lives inside each person who professes Christ, that she truly understood what it meant to be a Christian.

Her life is full of situations where God spared her from tragedy and included fourteen years of drug and alcohol abuse. But a gracious and loving God never took His hand from her. She can see today how He protected her even from herself.

My grace story is far different from Amy's but I'm just as gloriously saved. Like Amy's family, my family was at the church whenever the doors were open. They exposed me to the love of Christ from the time I was an infant and that showering and teaching never stopped. I came to know the Lord at the age of eleven after

CHAPTER TWELVE

growing up in Oakland Avenue Baptist Church in Catlettsburg, Kentucky, for my formative years. There are so many saints of God at that dear church who did disciple me after accepting Jesus Christ. They led by example and in word and deed. They showed and taught you how to walk with and grow in Christ.

I can remember the when and where as well. I was walking home from Charles Russell Elementary with a friend who went to church with me. As I was crossing the street at Blackburn Avenue and Division Street is when it really sunk in that I needed to be saved. Jesus had been working on me for weeks, if not years. We were having a revival at Oakland Avenue and it was Men's Night, where we had an all-male choir. My father, Clarence Maynard, was leading the singing, as he often did at the church. I can remember gripping the back of that pew when it came time for the invitation and then letting go and coming forward, a huge burden seemingly lifted from my young shoulders. I know it was a glorious day for my mother, Peggy, and my father. I hadn't told them I was considering coming forward.

I praise God today for a mother and father who understood the most important decision that my brother or I would ever make was accepting Jesus Christ as our personal Savior. They guided and directed our paths to that end and we both have enjoyed a lifetime of serving Him in various capacities.

My brother is an ordained minister and the senior pastor at Fruit Cove Baptist Church in Jacksonville, Florida, where he shepherds 4,000 members. I have served as a deacon at Unity Baptist Church for the past twenty-one years and in various offices within the church, including leading the music whenever called upon, just like my father did. My wife, Beth, has spent thirty-four years teaching in Christian education at Rose Hill Christian School. We have

A FINAL WORD

tried to serve God and be an example to others, including our children, Stephen and Sally, who are married adults now.

We praise God for His provisions in our life and praise Him for allowing us to be part of the Amy For Africa mission that has greatly impacted us both.

Praise God from whom all blessings flow!

CHAPTER THIRTEEN
AMY'S 2013 BOSTON MARATHON DIARY

FEBRUARY 18

I praise God for his awesomeness. One year ago today, I completed my first marathon. I can truly see how in just one year God has matured me as a runner but, most importantly, spiritually. He has opened doors and given me opportunities I never imagined. I praise him for his strength he provides in our weakness. Last week I ran nearly 55 miles while battling strep throat. Praise God for modern medicine. I got an antibiotic shot and felt much better within 12 hours and was able to run 12 miles.

Today, three days after receiving the medicine, I still felt weak during my 10-miler. I keep repeating 2 Corinthians 12. I actually ran one of my best 10 milers. It took 1:16:03, about a 7:36 per mile average and that included nine big hills! This is my "easy" week. I only have about 50 miles to complete. Real "easy."

FEBRUARY 19

The word to describe this run ... windy! Yes, the wind was

CHAPTER THIRTEEN

strong and had a good chill to it. Good run though; short five miles at 6:53 pace. Felt good except for the occasional wind burst. But it may be windy in Boston. So it's good experience and preparation is the key.

I worked midnights last night, had my 2-year-old today so going on about three hours sleep. I just tell myself it's preparing me to run through the fatigue of the marathon. God is good and supplies exactly what I need.

FEBRUARY 20

I felt tired today at work. Midnight shift last night. Slept good but today I could feel the fatigue setting in. As the miles keep building I can feel the fatigue building but, with all that, I cranked out one of my best 10-milers today, a 7:19 pace. I prayed most of my run. It really helps pass the time and keeps me focused on something rather than "how much longer?" Thankful to be done today and injury free!

FEBRUARY 21

Started my day at 4 a.m. with coffee, Bible, then running. Today was a little different, a sprint day. I logged seven miles total but the majority of the run was 7x800 meter sprints at a 6-minute pace. I do these workouts on the treadmill because it's impossible to slow down. I don't really enjoy sprinting but it is a necessity. I read in a running book written by a legend that "everyone knows how to run slow, the trick is learning how to run fast."

My goal with sprint workouts is to teach my body how to run fast for a long time. Today I would sprint a half mile, then jog a quarter mile, and did that for seven miles. I started my day at 4 a.m. because tonight is Disney on Ice with the family. Very excited. Had to get my workout in early because later wasn't an option.

AMY'S 2013 BOSTON MARATHON DIARY

FEBRUARY 22

Today was a nice easy six miles at a 7:30 pace. I couldn't go much faster with the ice storm that hit last night. It was as if someone had dumped small ice chunks every 10 feet. Not solid ice but patches and pieces everywhere. The trees were beautifully covered in a sheet of ice. It made me think of how truly beautiful God's creation is. There was also a rainy mist, which I enjoy to run in.

After the run it was off to the gym for strength training. It's an essential part of marathon training. Strength training builds your muscle and protects you from injury. The stronger the muscle the less likely you are to have an injury. It also gives you extra reserve during the race when your muscles start to break down. It's good to have some reserve to stay strong. Enjoyed the run today but glad it's over.

FEBRUARY 23

I worked last night 8 p.m. to 5 a.m. I came home and slept until 9:30 a.m. I just couldn't sleep anymore. I was excited about this evening where all the local church choirs were singing at the Paramount. I can't wait but first must get in 12 miles at race pace. I was shooting for 7:30/mile but halfway through my watch battery died. It was kind of nice though … just enjoying the run. I have been so focused on pace the last few weeks. I think it was God's way of saying "just take today and enjoy your run." So I did and pushed but focused more on finishing the miles.

This time of running freely gave me time to focus on what God is trying to tell me. In my Bible study this morning, God really spoke to me. I Timothy 4, 7-10 says: "Train yourself to be godly. For physical training (for me running) is of SOME value; but godliness

CHAPTER THIRTEEN

has value for all things ... and for this we labor and strive." It got me to wondering if I was as focused spiritually as I am on running? Running is only of SOME value but my relationship with Christ is invaluable. I'm laboring and striving to do my best in Boston, putting in mile after mile. Maybe I can learn and strive even more to be exactly what God wants me to be.

FEBRUARY 24

Rest day: The most important and beneficial day of the week.

FEBRUARY 25

I worked last night, 8 p.m. to 8 a.m. Despite only about three solid hours of sleep, I knocked out six miles at 6:52 pace. Felt good, felt strong. Even had a couple of good hills incorporated into the pace. Now preparing mentally and physically for tomorrow's 20-miler by increasing my caloric intake today. Increasing the carbs and mentally psyching myself up. I enjoy the long runs — challenging but always rewarding. At this point in the game the long runs are 90 percent mental, 10 percent physical. Philippians 4:13!!

FEBRUARY 26

Started day at 4 a.m. with coffee, Bible study and now running! I truly praise God for my run today. Twenty miles completed at 7:41 pace, including 13 big hills. My last hill was Ashland Avenue at mile 19 and the last mile was one of my fastest at 7:12. I felt good and strong and felt God's strength. I drank about 20 ounces of Gatorade during the run and ate some energy gummies at miles 8 and 17. It's amazing how something so gross can taste so wonderful when all you need is sugar/energy. Now my favorite part, recovery

AMY'S 2013 BOSTON MARATHON DIARY

… this is when I get to replenish all the carbs I burned. I basically get to and NEED TO eat every 2-3 hours all day — my favorite part of the long run.

FEBRUARY 27

I started my day at 4:30 a.m. I had the alarm set for 5 a.m. but couldn't sleep. Had my usual routine — coffee, Bible study, run! The time in God's word always comes before my run. I don't want to get my priorities out of order. God must come first … otherwise the rest will will fall part. Today was an easy, relatively flat, seven miles at 7:30 pace.

The weather was awesome; I actually ran in a tank top. I love how it's starting to warm up. Still had gloves and tights on but that's fine with me. Today was a recovery run. The point is not to go too fast but promote blood flow to the muscles that were broken down in yesterday's long run. The increased blood flow decreases soreness and increases the speed of recovery.

God has brought me so far in my running. Last year I would be so sore after a 20-mile run. But today only a little soreness in my hamstrings. Praise God for his goodness, love and faithfulness.

FEBRUARY 28

Excited today I got to try out my new running shoes … I think these will be my official Boston race shoes. This is the third pair I've gone through in the 18-week training. I broke them in with a good 10-miler at a 7:28 pace. I felt very tired. Worked last night and then had my 2-year-old today. I'm running on about three hours of solid sleep but got in my run and strength training.

God's convicting me today over my poor attitude during my

CHAPTER THIRTEEN

run. Every car on the road was irritating me — either drove too close, too slow, too fast, etc. I was just full of complaints then I suddenly was like, "God, please forgive me and my horrible attitude." I decided then to start counting my blessings and it's amazing how quickly my attitude changed. God is good all the time … That's how my focus needs to remain.

MARCH 1

Wow! Today was intense! I started with a 1 1/2-mile warmup, then off to Ashland Avenue for a strong hill-climbing session. Up and down Ashland Avenue continuously for five miles. Eight times total I went up Ashland Avenue and back down. It's very challenging both physically and mentally … but extremely beneficial for strength and endurance training.

I ended with a nice flat one mile cool down. I'll be honest, I had to call out to God a couple of times during the hill session. "Give me your strength Lord, give me your power." And yes God always supplies exactly what I need. Seven miles completed. Very thankful it's over and injury-free. What a way to spend Friday evening.

MARCH 2

Ten miles completed this morning at a 7:06 pace. One of my best runs! It was 28 degrees, flurries with a brisk chill in the air. I felt good and strong toward the end though I was praying for God's empowerment. I felt weak toward the last mile, called out to him and ran one of my strongest miles at 6:49 pace. Sixty miles completed this week by the grace of God. Feeling strong, enjoying my new shoes and counting my blessings.

AMY'S 2013 BOSTON MARATHON DIARY

MARCH 3

Rest day! Yea!! After this week's training I'm not sore but my legs feel tight and even my arms feel tight. I'm going to fully enjoy this rest day. Getting ready for church is about as active as I plan on getting! Church … nap … church. That's my plan!

MARCH 4

Today was cold. I checked the temperature before I went running and it was 21 degrees but it felt a little colder. I did a "short" long run, 12 miles at 7:40 pace. Since this week's long run was shorter, I wanted to challenge myself so I ran the hilliest court I could find. Incorporated 15 hills into this run anywhere between 100 meters to 800 meters in length! There was also rolling hills in between those.

At one point in the run I noticed small ice crystals that had developed in my eyelashes ... that means it's cold! I felt good and strong today! Praising God this is an "easy" week … only 50 miles to complete. Feeling energized from all the outpouring of love and support from my family, church family, friends and community. I truly appreciate everyone.

MARCH 5

I worked last night 8 p.m. to 4 a.m. — praise God for family! My mother-in-law kept Jarek so I could sleep a little longer. I woke up around noon and spent good quality time in God's word and prayer. Another Boston Marathon runner got in touch with me via Facebook today. We talked some about our training and excitement about the race but most of our talk was about how thankful we both are for our awesome spouses and supportive families. We both agree

CHAPTER THIRTEEN

we couldn't do it without them. God gives you exactly what you need when you need it. That's not only in racing but also in life and in the family and mate he gives you.

I ran five miles at a 7:00 pace. It was a nice recovery run — not too fast, not too slow. I could feel the fatigue from yesterday's hills. My legs felt heavy and I kept my focus on thanksgiving. I mentally went through a list of things I'm thankful for. It made the run pass by quickly and kept my focus where it needs to be — on God's goodness, grace and faithfulness.

MARCH 6

Today, despite having only 3 1/2 hours of totally uninterrupted sleep after working 8 p.m. to 8 a.m. last night, I woke up energized. I felt very comfortable today running. Eight miles completed at 7:03 pace. I did attempt to run in the 6:50 range but my body would not allow me. I think I'm still in recovery-mode from last week's 60 miles and the hills on Monday. So I just ran at a comfortable pace. I'm excited to go to church tonight. The midweek services are so uplifting and critical to keeping you on the right spiritual track.

I feel very thirsty today. Working midnights I find myself drinking too much caffeine and not enough water or sports drinks. My goal today is to increase my "good" fluids intake. In order to run a good race, you must have a "well-oiled machine."

MARCH 7

I slept so good last night, waking up energized at 5 a.m. I started my day as usual with coffee, Bible, prayer and running. I ran a nice flat six miles at a 6:54 pace. It was a good run. I did, though,

AMY'S 2013 BOSTON MARATHON DIARY

have to keep focused to keep my pace in the 6:50 range. I'm at the peak of my training, preparing for my longest run of 22 miles next week. The build to this point has been challenging and my body is feeling the fatigue. The fatigue makes it hard to push my pace but in the end it will all pay off. Hebrews 12:1: "Run with patience the race marked before you ... fix your eyes upon Jesus!" That's what I'm doing — fixing my eyes on Christ, knowing he knows what he's doing. I just need to remain patient and faithful. God is in control.

MARCH 8

Great run today, six miles at 7:12 pace, then to the gym for strength training, then I did another mile cool down. The first half-mile of the cool down was slow and comfortable but I finished strong with three 200-meter sprints at a 5:00 pace. I wanted to wake my legs up a little.

Training for a marathon is more about getting the miles in, not so much a lot of speed work. Waking up those "sprint" muscles felt great. And, yes, if you saw someone running in 25-degree weather this morning with shorts on, that was me. I had all intentions of just taking it easy and running on the treadmill today. But on my way to the gym I thought, "God blesses hard work. I must give it my all." I was in shorts and a jacket and that's what I had for the 25-degree weather. It was refreshing and after the first mile I was plenty warm. I honestly believe God wants me to give 100 percent at whatever it is he has given me to do. Whether it's being a parent, employee, church member, spouse or runner, I must give 100 percent. Colossians 3:23: "Whatever you do, work at it with all your heart, as working for the Lord, not for men." That means no shortcuts.

CHAPTER THIRTEEN

MARCH 9

What a beautiful day to run: Sunny, 62 degrees, clear skies … simply awesome. I ran a good comfortable 12 miles at a 7:23 pace. Loved the time running in a tank-top and shorts — I'm so ready for spring! God's creation is simply amazing. Praise God from whom all blessings flow!

MARCH 10

Yea! Rest day! Going to enjoy this day, fuel up on some good carbs for the upcoming week and take it easy. One thing I really learned this week … sometimes you must just step out in faith and trust God with the rest.

MARCH 11

I woke up at noon today (after working until 8 this morning) to such a beautiful day: 61 degrees, just a light misty rain — perfect running weather. Completed six miles at a 6:52 pace. Mentally preparing for tomorrow's 22-mile long run. This will be my longest run completed during training. After this week it will get progressively "easier" until race day … just got to make it through this week! I'm excited for tomorrow, ready for the challenge. Going to the Roadhouse tonight with family … can't think of a better place to carb load … gotta love those rolls! Through Christ, all things are possible! Seriously, if you really think about it … what's 22 miles to God? A meager drop in the bucket! God is my tower of strength. I got this! No … We got this!

MARCH 12

I must be honest, today was a long, hard and rough 22 miles.

AMY'S 2013 BOSTON MARATHON DIARY

Everyone has "off" days and this was one for me. Every mile seemed like two and my pace was hard to maintain. I finished with a 7:59 mile average and only by the grace of God. The last five miles I literally kept repeating a hymn: "I need thee, oh I need thee, every hour I need thee!" I was calling out to God for strength because I was weak and, of course, he supplied! Twenty-two miles completed and injury free. Praise God!

MARCH 13

Today I took it nice and slow for my recovery run: seven miles at 7:57 pace. After yesterday's tough 22-mile run, I haven't become discouraged but I did seek some advice from a good friend and awesome runner in John Davis. He is a former Marshall University runner and 2010 Boston Marathoner with a time of 2:46. He placed 279th out of 22,540 runners and he completed a 100-mile race so, needless to say, he is a very knowledgeable runner. He told me I may be at the point of overtraining — something all long distance runners are guilty of. It's the fine line between pushing yourself to the limit and overdoing it. So today I chose to really slow down the pace and allow for adequate recovery. I'm praying God gives me wisdom in my training. I'm glad it's still a month out; plenty of time to fully recover and run an awesome race.

I praise God for good friends once again. God has given me what I need exactly when I needed it. John has truly been an inspiration coach and friend to me. I know he doesn't even realize how greatly he has influenced my life. That's why it's so critical we all treat others with love because you never know how God is using you in another's life.

CHAPTER THIRTEEN

MARCH 14

Today I had to make the choice to do what I need to do instead of what I wanted to do. I only completed half my workout today. I got in five slow miles at 8:00 pace. Today I developed a nagging pain in my left lower calf. I immediately iced it when I got home. I am concerned. My pace is slow and injuries are starting to surface, but I am choosing to praise God anyway. God is so good to me. He knows exactly what's going on and I know he works for the good of those who love him. My hope is in Him. I'm praying for wisdom and God is telling me to rest. I chose to only do half the workout today and will take it day by day. Yesterday eight of the elite runners pulled out of the Boston Marathon due to injury. This part of the training either makes you or breaks you. I praise God for how far he's brought me. He's ultimately in control! May his will be done.

MARCH 15

After limping around all day yesterday and wrapping ice packs to my leg throughout the day and all night at work, I decided no running for today would be best. I did though cross-train 17 miles on the stationary bike set to rolling hills mode at level 10-12. I did incorporate 16 800-meter sprints on the bike and also did strength training. I rejoice in the Lord today because, after seven hours of solid sleep, I woke up with no limp. Praising God for his amazing love and compassion! God knows what I need. He is in control and I just pray his will be done in my life and pray for wisdom and his healing. God is so good all the time!

MARCH 16

Feeling very encouraged today! I was able to run four miles

at a slow pace but 99 percent pain-free. I also got in four miles on the bike pain-free. I'm trying to take it easy and promote healing and recovery. I am so thankful to the sweet couple who gave my husband a medicine horse trainers use on their horses when they are injured. It is wonderful. I put it on my leg last night and they feel 99 percent better this morning. I praise God that he brought this sweet couple and their "horse medicine" into my husband's life.

Once again, God gives you exactly what you need when you need it. He uses people in your life to bless you and in return we need to make it a point to bless others with our lives. God is amazing. He is in control. He is the Great Physician. He is faithful and he is good all the time! … Now off to Winter Jam for some true worship and praise time! Can't wait!!

MARCH 17

What a crazy week! I hit a few speed bumps in my training. It was a totally unexpected turn of events. This week's training was supposed to be my most intense week. I was to cover 62 miles but, instead, I completed 44 slow miles and 21 bike miles. I'm not going to lie, I shed a couple of tears this week in fear of not being able to complete my goals. But that fear only lasted a moment because fear is not from the Lord. I am not going to let this turn of events keep me from praising God. Whether I'm running or in bed with ice packs strapped to my body, God is still God and he deserves all my praise.

God is using these injuries, this "speed bump," to make me more like him. I could question God … "Why God, I have worked so hard. Why now, so close to race day?" … But there's no point in questioning my Creator, my King, my Loving Father. I knew the answer … "It's to teach you, to mold you, to make you more like me!"

CHAPTER THIRTEEN

Praise God he is always at work in us. Whether we understand our situation or not, we know He works for our good! Praise God from whom all blessings flow!

MARCH 18

Had a great run today! Not because I was fast or my best time ever but simply because the weather was a perfect 40 degrees and I was able to run. I ran 12 miles at a slow pace. My goal was to complete the run as pain-free as possible. I noticed when I would run less than an 8:30 pace I could feel my left calf start to get tight and hurt. I kept it slow and just enjoyed the fresh air and ran with joy!

American Marathon record-holder Ryan Hall says we should "run with joy" no matter the weather, time or what place we are in. There is so much to be thankful for, there is no reason, no matter what the situation, if you're running with God, you should always be running with joy!

My goal this week is healing and recovery. I'll take it day by day and listen to my body.

A good friend of mine and fellow Boston Marathon runner encouraged me today. He said, "The hay is already in the barn," meaning I have done all the work. At this point I have nothing left to do except heal up, rest and run my best race possible.

MARCH 19

Feeling so pumped and encouraged today. I ran six miles at a nice comfortable 99 percent pain-free pace of 7:30. I'm so excited and thankful because, literally less than one week ago, I was dragging my left leg behind me due to severe pain. I still though am cautiously going to not push my pace because I'm still healing! I'm just so thankful today. God is so good! He heals and he is amazing. I'm also thankful for the very encouraging emails I have received from local runners. Great advice has been given by these people. God has put them into my life to encourage me! I'm thankful for their kind words. It's amazing how a kind and encouraging word can boost your spirit and energy! Praise God for he is in control!

MARCH 20

Today was a good run: nine miles at a comfortable 7:21 pace. My left calf felt tight, no pain except for the end of my cool down and it was just a tinge of pain. I immediately strapped ice-packs to my left calf and elevated it up on some pillows. I still, though, feel encouraged. I feel that my leg is healing daily and not getting worse so I'm very excited for that.

The wind the past two days has been brutal; I almost lost my hat a couple of times. I have a feeling Boston is going to be windy and God's preparing me for that.

I just continually thank God for his love and healing power. Literally one week ago I was limping home in tears from pain and discouragement and today I ran smoothly and even incorporated a couple of hills into this run. God is so good, so powerful! I praise him for my health and healing!

MARCH 21

Today was a great day! Six easy miles on the treadmill at 7:28 pace and totally pain-free!! Very excited. I did choose to run on the treadmill today because it's easier on your legs. This weekend I have a six-mile hill climb to conquer so I wanted to promote full recovery today to prepare for that.

I know even though the pain is gone, I'm not fully healed, so

CHAPTER THIRTEEN

I still must take it slower and easier. I did strength training today, also pain free. I'm getting so excited for Boston ... 25 days away. It will be here before I know it. My family has decided to take on a small mission venture ... we want to pass out 1,100 gospel tracts while we are in Boston. With nearly 300,000 spectators and 28,000 runners we see an opportunity. We are praying and asking for others to pray that God will prepare the hearts of those who receive the tracts that they may come to know the Lord. My dad came to know Jesus Christ through a tract ministry so we firmly believe in it. We pray God is glorified and his word reaches those who need his salvation! To God be the glory!

MARCH 22

TGIF! After working the past four nights, I slept great today. I woke up around 2:30 p.m. Of course, started my day with coffee, Bible and a run! I felt great today running. I ran seven miles at 7:07 pace and, really, no pain, just a little tightness in my left calf toward the end. Praising God for restoration!

So excited today! All my siblings are in town and we get to hang out! Tomorrow I get to go support my two sisters and my husband at the Bobcat 5K. I would like to run it but not going to chance it with my injury. I'm not one to sign up for a 5K "just to run it." I want to compete and do my best. I'm afraid I'll pull my left calf if I try to compete. I'll really enjoy just going and cheering them on! God has truly blessed me with the best family and for that I am thankful.

MARCH 23

Praising God today for an awesome 99 percent pain-free hill

run. I started with a one-mile warmup and then ran 13th Street hill, the one that runs beside the tennis courts and ACTC — six miles I believe. It was 11 times total up and down that hill. I'm so excited because even though I did have a little tightness in my left calf, all in all I felt great! I then finished with 1-mile cool down! I praise God for how quickly he is healing me. Three weeks until race day! I'm starting to feel the nervous energy. I know God is going to carry me every step of the way!

Now off to the Bobcat 5K in Ironton where I get the pleasure of watching my two sisters and husband compete. It will be nice to support them and just take it easy. May God bless their run, may it be fast, fun and injury-free!

MARCH 24

Rest day! Yea! I'm so excited to have all my siblings, parents and step-parents at church with me today and then to lunch with everyone. I've had such a great weekend with everyone! This was my first week of the tapering, the part of my training where it gets progressively easier until race day. I'll be honest, I've enjoyed it. God has been so good to me this week. He has blessed my health and healing. He has let me spend great time with my family and now today I get to worship him with my whole family! What a blessing! God is so great and so awesome. Forty-eight miles completed this week.

MARCH 25

I worked last night so I didn't sleep real well today. I had Jarek all day so I got about three solid hours of sleep. Luckily, I only had to run five miles today. I ran five miles at a 7:20 pace. I felt great,

CHAPTER THIRTEEN

very relaxed and did not have any pain. I did feel a little tightening in my left leg so I am going to ice it tonight. The weather was chilly today, 38 degrees with snow flurries and some wind. I really enjoyed the run today.

I told my husband, in a weird way, I'm thankful for my injury because I was starting to get burned out. Burnout happens to me toward the end of each marathon training period. It's the few weeks before the race when you're so mentally ready to race but physically your body needs some rest and recovery time before race day. So you still have a good 130 miles left to get in. You start to just want them to be over so you can race. But now, since the injury, I'm not burned out but so thankful just to be able to run. The "bump in the road" changed my whole attitude and perspective. I'm just truly going to enjoy these last couple of weeks. Each run is a mile closer to Boston! I'm so excited! So pumped! God is so good!

MARCH 26

Today was my long run for this week. Ten miles completed at a comfortable 7:58 pace. That time also was with a bathroom break. For a runner, a bathroom break is not stop running and go use the toilet … nope, it was all with Mother Nature and leaves to wipe. I'm not too proud to tell this but all long distance runners have done it. During a marathon, you will see people run in the woods and back out several times throughout the race. Oh the joys of running! All in all, a great run. No pain, just some tightening in my left calf. Very excited for Boston! Can't wait! To God be the glory.

MARCH 27

Slept in today and it felt great! I woke up at 7:19 a.m. but that

AMY'S 2013 BOSTON MARATHON DIARY

sure beats 3 a.m. or 5 a.m. I didn't get my run in until about 3 p.m. and it went great — six miles at a 7:17 pace. It wasn't my best time but it was absolutely pain free. No tightness, no pain ... it was great! Being only two weeks out from getting an injury, I'm praising God for healing me! My God, Jesus Christ, is alive and active! Yes he died on the cross but he rose again three days later!! Praise God from whom all blessings flow! Praise God for his love! Praise God for his amazing grace!

I wrote yesterday about how simple and human I am (using the bathroom in the woods) and yet the King of Kings, Lord of Lords, Creator and Savior died for me! God is great all the time!

I'm excited for spring but most of all I'm excited for Easter! What a beautiful day to celebrate. To celebrate the one true God ... who is alive and active today. He loves, heals, restores and prepares us and is with us every step of the way!

MARCH 28

So today was a little rough. I worked last night, 8 p.m. to 8 a.m., had my 2-year-old all day ... so sleep today was very limited and I feel very tired. Today I had fartleks to do for my workout. A fartlek run is where you sprint 3-4 minutes and then jog one minute. I did this for five miles. It was a very intense workout. Today I feel like Satan is attacking me. I've got bronchitis, which made my run every difficult to get through, and our truck broke down. I locked the keys in my car. No sleep. Even my hairbush broke today, just snapped in two pieces. What a day! The stress just keeps mounting ... at least that's the way it feels. But praise God for his grace! He gives us the grace we need to handle whatever comes our way ... big or small! I honestly believe God has great things in store for each

CHAPTER THIRTEEN

of us if we don't allow Satan to distract us with these earthly problems. I'm just going to focus on Christ. As long as I'm doing what he wants, he will take care of the rest better than I could ever ask or imagine.

MARCH 29

Good Friday! Praise God for giving his only son, Jesus, as a sacrifice so that we may live together with him!

Today was such a great run. It was absolutely beautiful weather – a perfect 55 degrees and sunny. I was able to run in a tank-top and shorts. I ran six miles at a 7:02 pace with three big hills incorporated. Absolutely pain free, no tightness in my left calf, no discomfort at all! So thankful and excited! Seventeen days until Race Day! The nervous injury is starting to kick in. I can't wait! Until then, though, I'm just truly enjoying the great opportunity God has blessed me with. We made our official dinner reservation to Cheers in Boston yesterday. So thankful to get this great experience with most of my family!! Red Sox tickets purchased for Saturday before the race (on Monday). God is just so good!

MARCH 30

What a gorgeous day! Sunny and awesome 56 degrees when I ran today! Absolutely perfect running weather. I ran eight miles at a 7:36 pace and then it was off to the gym for strength training. I felt great today once again with no pain or discomfort! I'm healing quickly and, for that, I'm so grateful! God's creation this time of year is just so beautiful. I love the flowers blooming at the park, the clear blue skies and I love the smell of fresh-cut grass! I actually smelled that today during my run! If we just look around, we can't deny God is amazing. His creation is beautifully and wonderfully made. God is above all, in all and through all! I praise God for this perfect Easter weekend!

MARCH 31

Happy Easter Sunday! For me, today is a rest day – no running, just enjoying this beautiful day of celebration. I'm thanking Jesus Christ that Easter Sunday was not a rest day for him. No, instead, he arose and conquered the grave! He's alive!!! Praise God for his son Jesus, our way to him. Praise God for his love and grace! Praise God for he is active and alive! He is never resting, always working, for the good of those who love him.

APRIL 1

Today I can really feel the excitement and nervous energy for the race. I woke up feeling that way. Two weeks until race day! It's crazy to think next week I'll be in Boston. What I've worked so hard for the past 1 1/2 years is almost here!

With all the nervous energy in me all I wanted to do is go run today. I ran eight miles at a nice 7:29 pace. There were some hills incorporated in that pace and it felt great. I spent the first 40 minute of my run in prayer, going through my daily run prayer list. The last 20 minutes I focused on proper running form. Proper form uphill, downhill and on flat surface, staying relaxed, keeping my head up! People who don't run marathons don't understand the preparation that it entails. You don't just get up and run 26.2 miles. Everything matters — your form, your fluid intake, your nutritional intake the week before, the day before, that day, your pace, your rest the week before and day before, everything you do must be taken into consideration.

CHAPTER THIRTEEN

But really isn't this how our daily life should be? Everything we say, do or don't do should be taken into consideration. Would God be pleased? Does this bring glory to God? Do others see God in me? Each of us would achieve great things if we considered God in our every word and deed. Something to think about ... to God be the glory!

APRIL 2

Today was such a great day to run! Sunny, 48 degrees, no wind ... it was awesome. I started with a one-mile warmup and then ran three quick miles at a 6:41 pace. Then I ended with a one-mile cool down. I felt great on my run. It came very easy. No pain or discomfort. I am still battling sinus problems and bronchitis but that too is getting better!

Just praising God today that my pace is getting back to where it was before my injury. I'm thankful. I know it's only by his grace and healing! When I finished my run today all I could say was "Praise God!"

APRIL 3

Wonderful run today — six miles at a 7:26 pace. Felt easy, felt great. I am so excited for Boston! I'm so excited for God has totally blessed my training and health. I can see all the pieces coming together. My Bible verse this week was Ephesians 3:20: "Now to him who is able to do immeasurably more than all we ask or imagine, according to his power that is at work within us, to him be the glory ..." So inspiring and encouraging. It's exciting to think it's not me alone running the Boston Marathon. It's God's power working in me! The creator, the sustainer of life, he is the one giving me the power, the strength. To him be the glory! I praise God that he is able to do immeasurably more than we can do or imagine. He is amazing and so loving. His love is indescribable. He is in control and, for that, I'm grateful!

APRIL 4

I cannot believe it's Thursday, April 4. We literally leave in one week for Boston! I can't believe it's actually here! Today was a great run. I started with a 1.5 mile warmup, followed by a four-mile hill run. I ran up and down Ashland Avenue seven times, which equaled four miles. Then I did a one-mile cool down. This hill run was absolutely pain-free! I felt great and am very encouraged. I started getting things together today for our trip. I'm very excited and so extremely thankful God has blessed me with this awesome opportunity. May he be pleased and he alone be glorified!

APRIL 5

So thankful today for my health! Two more elite runners dropped out of the Boston Marathon due to injuries — one experiencing a calf injury, the other a groin injury. That easily could have been me. I'm so thankful for God's mercy, his healing and his restoration! Today was an easy day … a rest day. This is the first time in months that I've had two rest days in one week. I'm really enjoying the rest time. Eating lots of protein and carbs, getting my muscles prepared for what's to come.

Today is so beautiful. Sunny and 60 degrees! Even though I'm supposed to have complete rest today, Jarek and I went on a 1.5 mile walk. The weather is just too beautiful to stay inside. Used that mile and half to take time to praise God for all my blessings!

CHAPTER THIRTEEN

APRIL 6

What a beautiful day to run! It's 69 degrees, sunny and just a slight breeze. I completed seven miles at a 7:29 pace and then went to the gym for strength training. It's my last official strength training session before Boston. I felt great today and injury free. Nine days until race day! I'm so excited, so ready to take the long run for Christ. My last marathon in Dayton, Ohio, I could literally feel God carrying me in that run. It felt effortless. That's when you know it's the power of God carrying you through, when something that takes so much effort feels effortless. I can't wait until Boston. I can't wait to take this journey with him. It's going to be awesome!

APRIL 7

Rest day! Excited because tonight is my last shift at work and them I'm on vacation. It all seems so surreal. I can't believe in eight days it's race day! The last four months I've been training so intensely and now it's so close!

I can't find the words to express my thoughts and feelings now. It's just pure excitement, gratefulness, nervousness and happiness! I never dreamed how God would use this opportunity to draw me closer to him, how he would use this race to change my life. Before this experience I had prayed earnestly for God to make me a bold witness and to use my running as a ministry to him, to bring him the glory!

I have been saved since I was a little child but never really "walked the walk" or even tried until this past year. That's when God really started convicting me about being a "closet" Christian. Sure I would go to church on Sundays and Wednesdays but Monday through Saturday I lived just like the rest of the world. No one could

AMY'S 2013 BOSTON MARATHON DIARY

tell I was a Christian. Last July I told God, "Lord, I'm done living two lives. I want to live for you and you alone." Since then I have had so much peace, so much joy and I can just see God moving in my life.

I believe God truly wants to use every one of us in great ways … we just have to be willing and obedient. I praise God for how he's working in my life. There's lots of work left to be done but I just praise him for loving me and being so very patient with me! I praise God for giving me the opportunity to use my running as a platform to witness for him. I praise him for making me a bolder witness. I pray he continues to use my running and my passion for him. To God be the glory!

APRIL 8

Wow! One week out from Race Day! The excitement is getting intense. I went to my daughter Skylar's track meet today (where she did great, by the way) and it really made me ready to race. Before the track meet I had to get my workout in: Five easy miles at a 7:14 pace. I can tell my body is starting to get really rested up and recovered from the weeks of training because my times are getting faster but with less effort. I feel good, ready to race!

I started increasing my amount of "good" fluids today – lots of water and Powerade. I want to make sure I'm totally hydrated by Race Day. Also had a nice pizza and bread sticks tonight, increasing the carbs. This week my diet will consist of about 80 percent carbs. My muscles need to be fully loaded to perform my best.

I'm extremely excited today because I found out Team Hoyt will be running the Boston Marathon again this year. This marks the father/son duo's 31st year of running the Boston Marathon. This duo

CHAPTER THIRTEEN

is unique because the dad (Dick Hoyt) pushes his son (Rick) in a wheelchair all 26.2 miles. These men have even completed triathlons together. Rick Hoyt told his dad years ago he wanted to run a marathon. His dad told his wheelchair-bound son, "OK, let's do it!" Since then these men have competed in marathons and triathlons all over the country. They run because they love it.

This father/son relationship is beautiful and shows real love. You can't help but think of God's amazing love when you hear this story. If a mere man could love his child so much he would push him 26.2 miles, swim and pull him in a boat three miles and bike him 112 miles, we can't even comprehend the love God has for us. He sent his son, his ONLY son, to die for us so that we may live with him. Now that's real love. That's the kind of love we need to strive for. That's the kind of love we need to show! Praise God for his amazing love!

APRIL 9

Such a beautiful day! It's 84 degrees and sunny, just a slight breeze. My run today was great – six miles at an easy pace of 7:30. My body and mind wanted to go faster. I kept looking down at my watch and finding myself running in the 6:50's. I had to keep reminding myself: "Slow down, save it for Race Day!" I feel excited. My mind and body are ready to race!

My run today was interesting. I heard someone yell "Marathon girl!" and another person a little later said "Are you Boston?" and then on my cool down a sweet couple on their bikes said "Are you Amy?" To all these questions I waved and said "Yep!" I'm so thankful to this community for all the love, support and encouragement you have shown me through this journey! I'm very blessed to receive

AMY'S 2013 BOSTON MARATHON DIARY

such positive feedback from everyone whether by shoutouts on the road or by the awesome emails I've received. I want all to know your kind words are very encouraging and very helpful. I'm running first for God, second my family and thirdly for this area. This area has been some overcome with drug abuse. It doesn't have to be that way. I want to show with God's love, grace and power anything is possible! I can do all things through Christ who strengthens me. Philipians 4:13. … and so can you!

APRIL 10

I slept for almost 12 hours last night. Getting all the rest I can this week. I am just so excited today. One of the elite runners posted this morning on Facebook she felt like a little kid on Christmas Eve! That's exactly how I feel! Excited, full of wonder, just wanting to dig right in to the presents or, in my case, the race! Five days out and my heart is already beating a little faster! I read today in Matthew 28:20 where Jesus said "I am with you always." He didn't say sometimes, he said always. I have a peace about the race knowing God himself is right there with me! I'm not anxious at all. I have no doubts knowing God is with me every step, every mile, till the finish forever! Praise God for his faithfulness. He never leaves us! If we feel distant from him it's because we have left him! He's the same yesterday, today and forever!

This is my last journal entry from Kentucky. It's bittersweet. I've truly enjoyed sharing this journey, sharing God's love! Today is a rest day and that's what I intend to do.

It's off to Boston early tomorrow morning! My purse is loaded with 200 tracts for the journey from Columbus to Boston! To God be the glory!

CHAPTER THIRTEEN

APRIL 11

So today was very eventful. In view of running it was a rest day. But today was anything but restful. We left Ashland at 3 a.m., drove to Columbus, then from there flew to Washington, D.C., then to Boston. Every flight was on time and smooth sailing so we were very blessed! Once in Boston we had to figure out the subway and bus system - a huge task for eight kids and nine adults. But we did it and even made it to our dinner reservations on time. Of course, I had pasta and shrimp for dinner. Pretty much eating all carbs today! Bought some Twizzlers; those are great for carb loading. Low in fat and nearly 40 carbs per serving! I praise God today for our safe travels.

Praising God today because we got nearly 350 tracts passed out today! The kids were just so on fire to get God's word out! We adults have a lot to learn from them today. They were all so bold for Christ. They were rejected a few times but that did not stop them! It was just so beautiful, such a great moment in my life to see my kids, my niece and my nephew so on fire for God!!

I pray God gives me the boldness each of these children had today! God is so awesome and I praise him for my children and the fact that they all know him and love him! To God be the Glory!

APRIL 12

Awesome day! I woke up to fried potatoes and biscuits with strawberry jelly, thanks to my dad. A great start to the official first carb-loading day. We spent most the day at the marathon expo. Today was the first of three day expo. It was awesome. I picked up my bib (my race number) also received my official Boston Marathon racing shirt. It is very nice. The expo was like a runner's paradise. Every athletic brand was there with all their apparel, every sports drink and energy bar brand was there, too. We got to sample several different types of endurance foods. Also got a few nice Boston running shirts at a great price.

My favorite part of the expo was meeting Team Hoyt, the men I mentioned earlier in the week. They are the father/son duo who race together. The son has been wheelchair bound since birth and they have been in more than 1,000 races together. It was such an honor to shake their hands and just tell them how truly inspiring they are. Dick Hoyt, the father, is 72 and his son Rick is 51! Dick has pushed Rick in every race since they started in 1977! How awesome are they to still be marathoning together! They are very nice men! It totally made my day!!

After the expo we went for pizza and bread sticks (more carbs) and throughout the day I snacked on Twizzlers and drank five bottles of Gatorade, two bottles of water and my regular coffee and pop! All day I had some type of carb in my hand! I would just like to praise God today for blessing me so richly! For not only allowing me to run Boston but that I also got to meet the two most awesome runners I've heard of and got to experience all this greatness with my family! Just found out tonight my other sister from Chicago and her family will be here tomorrow night! Twenty-two people in one house! Eleven children and eleven adults! Wow... GOD is so good!! I absolutely have the best family and support group!!! Two more days till race day!!

I did run today, just four easy miles through Boston! I did notice this place is all city but very hilly. Lots of rolling hills! Hopefully Ashland Avenue has got me well prepared. We will soon find out!!!

CHAPTER THIRTEEN

APRIL 13

Again what an awesome day! We started the day off with a big breakfast at a local cafe... absolutely delicious! I had three large blueberry pancakes, great start to day 2 of the carb loading! Again today I've had some sort of carb with me all day. I ate one bag of Gummy Life savers and one bag of Swedish fish. That was an easy 600 carbs right there! I had three 32 ounce bottles of Gatorade and one bottle of water, that's of course on top of my regular fluid intake. For dinner I had a chicken sandwich, two orders of fries and a banana chocolate frappe. The frappe was voted "Boston's Best" in 2012 so I had to try it. For night snack I had Twizzlers and pretzels plus more Gatorade.

The simple sugars are what I'm wanting the most because they break down into energy the quickest!! Carbs, carbs and more carbs! We saw the Boston Red Sox play today, it was great! Fenway Park was awesome, so much history there. We also walked around downtown Boston a little. It's so unique and historic. I love it. Such a culture shock!

The atmosphere here is so exciting! Everyone is so pumped for the race. Not just the runners but even all the locals. People here love the marathon and all the runners! God has blessed me and my family so richly! One day out from race day and I'm feeling great. No pains, no aches! I feel fueled and ready to rock! Tract mission is going great! Total tracts passed out so far... 700!!! We know God's word will not return void so we are just passing them out all over! God is so awesome! Everyone needs to hear about him!!! I get to watch my husband and sister race in the Boston 5k in the morning! I pray God blesses them with a safe, fast, injury free and fun run! Can't wait to watch them!! Praising God today because he has

AMY'S 2013 BOSTON MARATHON DIARY

blessed my family and I more than we could ever have imagined! God truly is so good all the time! To God be the Glory!

No running today, just resting and getting fueled up!

APRIL 14

So today was incredible. Got to watch Amanda (my sister) and Chris (my husband) run the Boston 5K! They did awesome. The men's London Olympian silver medalist won the 5K at a time of 13:37! Yes 13:37... that is not a typo! It was awesome!

My family took the kids AND allowed me and Chris to go back to the expo by ourselves. It was amazing. I got to meet, shake hands with and have pictures taken with my favorite athletes and Olympians! Feel so very blessed today. God even got us to the front of both lines to meet them! He just totally worked it all out!

Since today is the day before Marathon Monday, no running for me! I focused on rest and carbs today! I ate a bagel, two pieces of toast, four rolls and 32-ounce bottle of Gatorade just for breakfast, then 12-inch calzone for lunch. Snacks in between! Tonight I will just eat light so I don't feel full in the morning.

Please say a prayer for me as soon as you read this. My starting gun is at 10:20 a.m. I'm excited and so very thankful! God has blessed me beyond belief and I know he'll carry me every step, every mile tomorrow! I can do all things through Christ who strengthens me! BOSTON 2013! TO GOD BE THE GLORY!!!!

END NOTES

FAMILY ONLY MINUTES FROM TRAGEDY

[This story appeared in the April 15, 2013 edition of The Independent. It is being reprinted with permission.]

BOSTON — For most of the day, 21 members of Amy Compston's family sat cramped at the Boston Marathon finish line.

They arrived early — about 6:40 in the morning — for prime positioning to watch Compston, the 28-year-old Ashland woman who is a fulltime nurse, wife and mother to four children finish the race of a lifetime.

Compston crossed the finish line only 30 minutes before a pair of explosions turned the Boston Marathon's finish line into a war scene. Amy's husband, Chris, was with her in the Boston Marathon's family meeting spot while her children, parents, siblings and their spouses had left the area only a few minutes before the explosions.

As soon as the race was over, Amy was ushered through an area for the runners and taken to the zone where she could meet family members. Her husband had to navigate through several Boston streets over about a 15-minute walk to get to where he could meet.

Meanwhile, the family was still at the finish line area awaiting word from Amy and Chris.

"We couldn't get a hold of them for the longest time," said her sister, Amanda Evans. "We finally did and she told us to meet at the train station so that's where we headed. We went around the corner to bypass traffic and heard the explosion."

Evans said "it really sounded like thunder but not in the sky or two trains hitting." She said they were too far away to hear anyone

END NOTES

screaming or the chaos that was about to ensue. "We kept walking. I'm saying we were like five minutes from that spot. We walked away (from the finish line), went the next alley over and we heard it.

"It was a God thing. He was watching over us. She (Amy) couldn't come to us so we had to come to her."

Evans said once all the family was together again, including Chris and Amy, they all breathed a sigh of relief although still prayerfully remembering those who were hurt from the explosion.

"Once we knew everyone of our group was OK and back together, we were good," she said. "You kind of get shaken, a little freaked out. We felt so bad for those people and their families. To have something so unexpected happen like this is awful."

Chris Compston said the day was "pretty exhausting" but well worth it. They waited eight hours at a crowded finish line area, he said.

"People were pushing you and would steal your spot," he said. "I had kids crying, hungry, thirsty, changing diapers... it was pretty tiring. But it got really exciting when the finishers started coming in. Then they just kept coming and coming."

Chris said they were tracking Amy's run through a Boston Marathon app and knew about when she would finish. He positioned himself to take a photograph "about 15 minutes early. You have a small window of opportunity. I didn't want to miss it in case she had a burst of energy."

Once she crossed the finish line, race officials kept her going while Chris had to find his way to the family meeting area.

"I went down three blocks, over three blocks, up four blocks and over two more," he said. "It took me 15 minutes of walking to get to where I could find her."

They finally met up and a woman runner asked Amy if she

END NOTES

could use her cellphone to text her husband. That's when they first found out about the explosions. Of course, their immediate thoughts went to family.

"My first thought was 'Did my family get away?' They were standing at the finish line," he said. "Have they left yet? Then Amy was talking to them and said everybody was OK. That was a relief."

"When the woman gave us the phone she said 'Did you hear what happened?' I thought it was a fight or something. She told us there were two explosions."

Chris said he felt sympathy for the many who were injured and the 12,000 runners who didn't get to complete the marathon. "I'm sure their families didn't know where to find them."

Amy Compston's sisters, mother and father, children and husband and cousins were among the 22 total family members, including Amy, who made the trip.

They took along with them several thousand Christian tracts and passed out many of them in the last days in Boston.

Evans and Chris Compston also experienced the Boston Marathon 5K

"The 5K was awesome," Amanda said. "The last mile was the same one Amy ran to the finish line today. I thought how I would feel if I was a marathoner and there was one mile left. People were cheering us on from beginning to end."

Chris Compston said the overall experience, from the year's worth of training to the experience in Boston, has been unbelievable.

"From the platform that she's been given, from public speaking to writing (in the newspaper), it's been unreal. Those are things she never thought she would do. Even coming to Boston has been great. The whole trip has been awesome."

END NOTES

MARATHON RUNNER: 'GOD SPARED US'

[This story appeared in the April 23, 2013 edition of The Independent. It is being reprinted with permission.]

FLATWOODS — Amy Compston, the local marathoner who finished the Boston Marathon about 30 minutes before the two explosions last week, said she and her family escaped injury only through God's grace.

She originally thought she finished only 22 minutes before the first explosion, but later learned it was closer to 30 minutes.

Her family members, who were lined up at the finish line between where the two bombs detonated since 6:30 that morning, had left the area only five minutes before the bombs went off.

In Compston's mind, that was no coincidence.

"God had his protection on us," she said, showing a photograph of the family members who were in Boston. "He has work for us to do. Eleven of our family members were children and the bombs were made to hit low. God spared us."

Compston, 28, gave a sometimes emotional talk to the East Greenup Kiwanis Club on Tuesday at its weekly meeting.

Compston finished among the top 15 percent of women runners and the top 23 percent overall in the world-famous race that attracted 23,000 runners. Her time of three hours, 27 minutes and 54 seconds was her personal best. She said the training on the hills of the area, including Ashland Avenue and 13th Street, prepared her for the hilly course in Boston.

"The hills are where I passed everyone," she said. "He pre-

END NOTES

pared me. I was on fire on those hills.

"I asked God for wisdom as I trained for the hills. I would run up and down Ashland Avenue six and seven times and on the road beside ACTC 11 times up and down."

Compston, who wrote a daily journal for The Independent in the eight weeks leading up to the Boston Marathon, gave an often emotional testimony about younger days before detailing what happened during the race. She talked about her bouts with drugs and alcohol and how God saw fit to spare her.

She plans to use her running as a platform to bring people to Christ. Her family distributed 1,200 Bible tracts at the marathon last week. One of those tracts was spotted in a crime scene photo near where the explosion had blown off someone's foot.

"I'm not the best runner in the world, but it's a gift he's given me," Compston said. "He trusted me with the opportunity to write the articles in the newspaper and to run for him. He's not done with me."

Compston, who has four children and works full time as an ER nurse at King's Daughters Medical Center, gave her husband, Chris, credit for being there for her.

"I have an awesome husband who sacrifices a lot," she said.

She said even though many of her family members heard the bombs, they were in the opposite direction from the chaos in downtown Boston.

"All of them heard it, but the peace that God gave us was amazing," she said. "We went and toured Boston the next day."

During her last two weeks of training, Compston said she made a promise to God she would run an ultra-marathon and take donations for two Penne Paris Memorial schools in Uganda. Ultra-

END NOTES

marathons are 50 miles (a regular marathon is 26.2). She will begin training in July for the November race in Nashville.

"I said, 'If I don't get injured in Boston, I'm going to do it,'" she said.

Compston said she would release more information about how to donate to the ultra-marathon at a later date. Or, she said those interested may email her amylwesolowski@yahoo.com

Despite all that happened, Compston said she plans to return to Boston next year. Her time already qualifies her for the race.

"All my family is on board, too," she said.

The Kiwanians invited Compston to participate in their 36th annual "Run by the River" 10K on June 8 — and even waived her entry fee.

Compston agreed to run, saying she uses 5Ks and 10Ks for "sprint work."

Amy Compston with her family in Ashland, Ky.: sons Elias (far left) and Jarek (on her lap) and daughters Bailee (left) and Skylar. She has full support of her husband, Chris, on her work with missions to Uganda through her running.